What are they saying about
A LITTLE BOOK ON JOY . . . ?

"Matthew Harrison takes the subject of joy and succinctly brings it into clear view. Something that any "dyed in the wool" Christian—even a staunch German Lutheran—can grasp and embrace. The book provides a fresh and honest look at how and why joy is an integral part of one's life."

CHERI FISH
PRESIDENT—MICHIGAN DISTRICT LWML

"A singular contribution! Matt Harrison's *A Little Book on Joy* is a big book in great need today. In his characteristically incisive manner, Matt has given today's Christian the keys to real joy—the kind the Savior intended, and the kind he created in his life, death, and resurrection. I commend it to all as a healthy antidote to the travails of modern life. Matt continues to be one of the most interesting, topical, and important authors on today's theological scene."

LEO MACKAY
VICE PRESIDENT—CORPORATE BUSINESS DEVELOPMENT
LOCKHEED MARTIN CORP.
PAST DEPUTY SECRETARY OF VETERANS AFFAIRS, WASHINGTON D.C.

"Let's face it: serious Lutherans too often come across as dour sourpusses. *A Little Book on Joy* shatters that caricature. Matt Harrison leads readers on an exuberant romp through the Scriptures and the multiple facets of unbridled Christian joy."

REV. HAROLD L. SENKBEIL, STM, DD
EXECUTIVE DIRECTOR, DOXOLOGY: THE LUTHERAN CENTER
FOR SPIRITUAL CARE AND COUNSEL

"Having come from a poor country in Asia and having seen people in poverty and misery my whole life, it always puzzles me to see many people in the United States who do not seem to have joy in their affluence. This book by Matthew Harrison is the answer to that mystery: true joy comes from God, and that joy of the Lord permeates our whole life. He also makes very clear that "joy" is not the same as "happiness," which depends on happenings and our circumstances. I wish everybody would read this book and be blessed by it."

KHAT KAHM
MYANMAR

"Wow! With *A Little Book on Joy*, Rev. Harrison touches at the heart of what is lacking in our sin-saddened world—joy at the foot of the cross for every aspect of our Christ-centered vocations. A must-read for God's people and church workers alike. Well done!"

REV. JOHN WILLE
PRESIDENT—SOUTH WISCONSIN DISTRICT, LCMS

"There is nothing 'little' about this book! With all of the theological prowess and doctrinal integrity one would expect from this colleague in ministry and friend, herein lies a manual—a workbook, if you will—on joy. For those seeking more joy in their life, or simply yearning for words to describe what they already know in their lives to be true, this very 'large' book looms as resource and inspiration. Thanks, Matt!"

REV. RICHARD A. NELSON
SENIOR PASTOR—CENTRAL LUTHERAN CHURCH (ELCA)
MINNEAPOLIS, MINNESOTA

"Do we need joy? Yes, indeed, we need joy as much as life, faith, and hope. . . . Matt Harrison takes us to Christ through his cross, his death, and his resurrection to show us true joy. Just as John writes, 'We are writing these things so that our joy may be complete" (1 John 1:4), so Matt enriches us with *A Little Book on Joy*. It takes us from where we are to where God would have us in his joy."

CHARLES L. MANSKE,
FOUNDING PRESIDENT—CONCORDIA UNIVERSITY IRVINE

"The poet William Wordsworth provided the verse which became the title of the writer C. S. Lewis' memoir: 'Surprised by joy—impatient as the wind.' . . . Joy is so often confused with happiness, or with contentment. Joy is neither, as Matthew Harrison shows so brilliantly in his *A Little Book on Joy*. This little, powerful, three-letter word needs to be in the working vocabulary of every follower of Jesus Christ. There is no better place to find joy than here."

TIMOTHY GOEGLEIN
VICE PRESIDENT FOR EXTERNAL RELATIONS—FOCUS ON THE FAMILY
FORMER SPECIAL ASSISTANT TO PRESIDENT GEORGE W. BUSH
AND DEPUTY DIRECTOR OF THE WHITE HOUSE OFFICE OF PUBLIC LIAISON

"This timely, refreshing, and much-needed 'little book' celebrates biblical joy, not worldly happiness. It is clear from the beginning that Rev. Matt Harrison has experienced the joy of which he writes, he understands it theologically, and he communicates in winsomely. Drawn from the fountain of joy that is the Gospel of Jesus Christ, *A Little Book on Joy* will truly help readers understand and live 'a good news life in a bad news world.'"

DR. JAMES I. LAMB
EXECUTIVE DIRECTOR—LUTHERANS FOR LIFE

"Matthew Harrison has done what I have always longed to do. He has written a lovely little book on joy. It may be little in size. Yet it is large in its impact, since it enlarges our spirits and their all-too-limited capacity for enjoyment. He shows how joy is the mark of a Christian. It taps out the rhythm and provides the tune for the life of faith in Christ. While happiness comes and goes, joy lasts. It is eternal, a foretaste of heaven here on earth. So in Philippians 1:25, Paul speaks about faith as a journey; for as we progress in faith, we progress in joy—abounding and increasing joy in Christ. As Harrison notes, we go from joy to joy, joy over joy, more and more joy. I commend this joyful book to you for your enjoyment and delight."

REV. DR. JOHN KLEINIG
AUSTRALIAN LUTHERAN COLLEGE

"Somehow we have forgotten the value of a joyful countenance. For some strange reason we have lost the fun in this life of faith . . . the contagious magnet of inner happiness has grown weak. Rev. Harrison helps us regain the joy by elevating Jesus who is the 'joy of the world.'"

THE REV. DR. BRYAN R. SALMINEN
SENIOR PASTOR—EMMANUEL LUTHERAN CHURCH
CADILLAC, MICHIGAN

"Matthew Harrison shares with us a contagious word of Good News, just what we all need to hear, often, regularly, constantly. 'Be of good cheer, I have overcome the world,' is what our dear Lord and Master tells us. His blessed Apostle St. Paul says, 'Rejoice in the Lord, always, and again I say, rejoice.' But this joy is not some whispy flight of fantasy, some elusive dream. It is real and solid, sure and certain because it is anchored in the One who loved us and gave himself up for us. He is our joy. This book explains why and how. Enjoy!"

PETER T. MCMANNIS
PUBLICIST AND HUMANITARIAN

"After finishing *A Little Book on Joy,* the reader will have discovered yet another joy: a work that combines Christ-centered theology with a refreshing, playful style. En-joy!"

REV. TERRY CRIPE
PRESIDENT—OHIO DISTRICT, LCMS

"Harrison has a knack for addressing pressing issues under the overall theme of joy: marriage stress, worship wars, euthanasia and abortion, intelligent design, depression in clergy, and church fellowship. A focus on joy, and not only law or 'Bible rules,' helps people see the beauty of life as God intends. Confessional Lutherans will benefit from God's richer blessings of joy, with a resulting optimism for both personal and church life."

BRYAN GERLACH
DIRECTOR, WELS COMMISSION ON WORSHIP

"Let the rich themes of biblical theology, as delightfully presented by Pastor Harrison, put joy in your heart—not the superficial happiness of pop entertainment, but the well-founded and deeply grounded joy that comes from God the Father through his Son Jesus Christ and in his Spirit."

DR. PAUL R. RAABE
PROFESSOR OF EXEGETICAL THEOLOGY
CONCORDIA SEMINARY—ST. LOUIS, MISSOURI

"Joy! It was a joy to read my friend's book. The first time I met Matthew, he started his 'talk' by strumming the banjo. The more he spoke, the happier the LWML ladies became. Just being around this talented man brought joy to my heart. Now I know the real secret to that joy!"

MARTHA P. BERGERON
PAST PRESIDENT—MID-SOUTH DISTRICT LWML

"When the world is too much with us, when our spirits are depressed, when pessimism and doubt control our thoughts, when fear perforates our hearts, Pastor Harrison's *A Little Book on Joy* helps us discover courage and purpose, peace of mind and heart, reason to rejoice—a new joy for our daily lives and service."

REV. DR. DONALD J. FONDOW
PRESIDENT—MINNESOTA NORTH DISTRICT, LCMS

"Pastor Harrison provides a down-to-earth and thoroughly enjoyable approach to a common dilemma faced, at one time or another, by every Christian: why don't I always feel joyful? ... A timely work, this book leads us to the only source of certain joy in uncertain times: the Good News of Christ and his Gospel."

DARIN STORKSON
ASIA DIRECTOR—LCMS WORLD RELIEF AND HUMAN CARE
JAKARTA, INDONESIA

"To the people of our age, joy and religion just do not seem to go together. There are so many things that get in the way—cares, concerns, burdens, fears of all kinds, and not least, all the troubles around the world. There seems to be no room for joy. . . . Pastor Harrison's book places before us genuine joy to show us whence it comes, from whom it comes, and how it works. He sets joy before us and invites us to receive it anew. *A Little Book on Joy* is indeed an exultation of joy divine."

REV. DR. DARIUS PETKUNAS, TH.D.
KLAIPEDA, LITHUANIA

"Excellent biblical meditations on joy, adorned with further reflections by many great thinkers of the Church, and made further accessible by fine discussion questions."

ROBERT BENNE
DIRECTOR—ROANOKE COLLEGE CENTER FOR RELIGION AND SOCIETY

"Deep, contemplative, a rich diet of Gospel in this little study on joy for the joy-less soul. I thought of others who in my estimation needed this little read on joy . . . and then I realized that I needed it too."

REV. RANDALL L. GOLTER
PRESIDENT—ROCKY MOUNTAIN DISTRICT, LCMS

"Make no mistake, this is no wishful-thinking, 'how-to' book that belongs shelved in the generic 'spirituality' section of the bookstore. Instead, this little book comes packed with a meaty message that reminds us of what true Christian joy really is. . . . By examining the deep roots of joy—its DNA, really—Rev. Harrison helps us see clearly how the presence of Christ and his mercy is woven tightly through a joy-filled existence."

MAGGIE KARNER
DIRECTOR OF LIFE AND HEALTH MINISTRIES
LCMS WORLD RELIEF AND HUMAN CARE

"'Where Christ is, there is joy,' says Luther. Christ Jesus is with us all the way—even in the sewer, Luther was bold to assert. . . . With self-effacing humor and keen attentiveness to the Holy Scriptures, Pastor Harrison is a wonderful tour guide to the places where the good Lord shows up bringing with him joy in the midst of sadness. Harrison demonstrates that Lutheran theology is a theology of joy unbridled and free on account of Christ. Enjoy these Christ-soaked pages!"

REVEREND JOHN PLESS
CONCORDIA THEOLOGICAL SEMINARY
FORT WAYNE, INDIANA

"We were taught in the Soviet Union that Christians were the saddest people on earth, hoping only for joy in the afterlife. And yet, Jesus said that he came so that his disciples may have life and have it abundantly. Somehow Rev. Matthew Harrison has gotten to the very core of Christianity in this easy-to-understand yet very instructive book."

BISHOP VSEVOLOD LYTKIN
SIBERIAN EVANGELICAL LUTHERAN CHURCH

"'Joy to the world, the Lord is come' is intoned all over the world during the Christmas season by the faithful commemorating the pivoting of all time and history in Bethlehem. . . . This 'Joy to the world' is the central message of Rev. Harrison's beautiful little booklet, provoking its readers to join the joyful sound of happiness, delight, and bliss praising God's grace and mercy which is new every morning."

REV. DR. WILHELM WEBER
BISHOP ELECT—LUTHERAN CHURCH OF SOUTH AFRICA

"To 'rejoice with joy'—that's how the Baptist put it when he heard the Bridegroom's voice. Through a wonderful association of illustrations by Kurt Onken, apt quotations and anecdotes, and simple yet profound reflections on the realities of faith and life, Matt Harrison has produced a 'little book' on a central gift of salvation. *A Little Book on Joy* is so well done and reads so easily. What a great book for young and old, for the catechumen, and for the more mature in faith!"

WILLIAM C. WEINRICH
RECTOR—LUTHER ACADEMY
RIGA, LATVIA

"The Gospel makes us optimists: 'If God be for us, who can be against us?' (Romans 8:31). Yes, life brings suffering, sin, and pain, ending in death, but God gives joy! Sometimes it is a laughing-out-loud, beyond-belief surprise; at other times he gives a quiet, sustaining joy in the face of the worst circumstance. But joy always comes in Christ, given for us. In him, God receives us, forgives us, and gives life. Matt Harrison brings out this joy in a book that's both accessible and fun for everyone. It's going to be a truly great book!"

REV. HERB MUELLER
PRESIDENT—SOUTHERN ILLINOIS DISTRICT, LCMS

"Pastor Harrison writes both faithfully and merrily, having first received joy himself. He knows that joy is not something to be forced on others. Nor is it something to be feigned for others' sake. This little book takes all the 'don't worry, be happy' clichés and throws them out the window. It frees the reader to recognize genuine joy—even on bad days and even in the midst of a bad news world."

DEACONESS ROSE E. (GILBERT) ADLE

"Pastor Harrison's book is a most helpful antidote against the plague of utilitarianism that shapes our post-modern age and that has had a destructive impact on the Church, as can be seen in many trends of Christian spirituality and piety. The author's inspiring, Gospel-oriented approach opens the reader's eyes to the multitude of divine gifts even in our fallen world (creation, family, marriage, humor) and in the realm of Christ's Church."

DR. ARMIN WENZ
PASTOR—ST. JOHN'S LUTHERAN CHURCH
OBERURSEL, GERMANY

"This little book of joy is needed. It is refreshing to rediscover that there is 'joy in the mud.' It was particularly uplifting to hear Luther the pastor speaking through the carefully selected quotes. It was helpful to reflect on laying down personal burdens and taking up the burdens of others in the community of joy, the Church. I found it enjoyable to read, and I commend it to you for your encouragement and enjoyment."

DR. ANDREW PFEIFFER
AUSTRALIAN LUTHERAN COLLEGE

"From Matt's own life stories, true to this book's purpose; you will discover how to find joy that is of God alone, amid the timeless biblical stories of the Trinitarian God coupled with your own stories of life. Matt teaches you how. The discovery of joy, previously unnoticed and uncelebrated, will be yours in the reading this timely little book. A good choice, too, for small faith-sharing groups!"

REV. JOHN H. DELANEY
PASTOR—ST. CATHERINE OF SIENA CATHOLIC PARISH
SOUTH BEND, INDIANA

"Frankly, I've grown weary of being lectured on joy. I'm also tired of that 'left behind' feeling that comes from listening to believers talk of joy in breathy tones that often don't sound true to life. It's one thing to speak about joy, when what I really need is Jesus. This book, with tales of the kinds of things we all experience and oozing with words from God, can help you. It brings Jesus near. Read this book. It will be rich time well spent."

ROBERT BUGBEE
PRESIDENT—LUTHERAN CHURCH CANADA

"This book has the makings of a devotional classic. Drawing on his keen insights into Scripture and his rich personal experiences, Rev. Harrison discloses the joy that is at the beating heart of the Christian life. Not that he minimizes the crosses, the trials, and the failures that we all know too well. Rather, he shows how we can 'live a good news life in a bad news world' because the Gospel of Christ transfigures everything."

GENE EDWARD VEITH
PROVOST—PATRICK HENRY COLLEGE
DIRECTOR—THE CRANACH INSTITUTE

"'When you preach the Gospel, people should tell from your looks that it is joyful news! Don't you get it?!' So Professor Holsten Fagerberg shouted grimly to us candidates for the ministry, while looking as though he had just swallowed a liter of vinegar. Every page of Harrison's book reverberates, not with a forced or put-on smile, but with the joy that God himself gives us in the kingdoms of nature and of grace. This is a useful book."

REV. FREDRIK SIDENVALL
PRINCIPAL—LUTHERAN HIGH SCHOOL
GOTHENBURG, SWEDEN

"Matthew Harrison has ventured into the topic that is the goal of our faith, for joy is what God expected from his creation, especially in man. Harrison reveals that joy is a gift. . . . This book is a real inspiration also to us in Africa, where we face so many challenges—to explore the joy we have from God, and to share it with our neighbors, i.e., the joy of the Gospel."

BISHOP WALTER E. OBARE
EVANGELICAL LUTHERAN CHURCH IN KENYA

"The angel brought Good News of great joy to the world (Luke 2:10) and announced the birth of Christ. This joy is for the entire world. There is no barrier of color, caste, or creed. . . . Sadly, this joy is still missing in the community and even the Church. But if we lack it, how are we going to show forth this joy, especially in countries like India, where there are such challenges to spreading the Good News of Christ? I deeply appreciate the efforts of Rev. Harrison in writing this book and hope that this 'little book' will brighten many hearts with great joy!"

REV. J. SAMUEL
PRESIDENT—INDIA EVANGELICAL LUTHERAN CHURCH

"'. . . if it is to be a life which knows true joy, it shall be a joy in perspective'—so writes Matthew Harrison and, indeed, perspective is the strength of *A Little Book on Joy*. Harrison teases out biblical moments of joy, translates them to our everyday lives, and in lively prose provides glimpses of the delights God promises. Joy abounds, and still he makes it clear that the most profound joy is when we know our need of God and know that God fulfills all his promises. This book is centered in the clear understanding that human sinfulness and God's remarkable grace is at the heart of the story."

JILL A. SCHUMANN
PRESIDENT AND CEO
LUTHERAN SERVICES IN AMERICA

"This book makes clear the mission of the Lutheran Church going forward. Through his recognition of Lutheran missionaries like Nommensen, Harrison presents a formula for the continuation of Christ's mission on earth. Harrison sees the mission of God's Kingdom as very relevant and open to all nations. This book calls and challenges all saints in Christ's Church to celebrate their joy in the love of God, showing why the Lutheran Church must be an evangelical church. Harrison's attention to and understanding of Lutheran churches around the world shows him for the true Lutheran leader that he is."

REV. NELSON SIREGAR
EXECUTIVE DIRECTOR—DEPTARTMENT OF DIAKONIA
HKBP, INDONESIA

"Our ominous times seem to confirm day after day Luther's earthy observations about the fetid character of pusillanimity. Thus there could not be a more propitious moment for the delicacies on the rich Trinitarian menu of joy offered up by Matthew Harrison. In this wonderful narrative, he reminds us that the Greek words for joy and grace used in the Bible are etymological siblings. This is an enchanting little book that makes us smile from page to page, and is wholesome balm for souls succumbing to faintheartedness."

UWE SIEMON-NETTO PH.D., D.LITT.,
DIRECTOR—CENTER FOR LUTHERAN THEOLOGY & PUBLIC LIFE
CONCORDIA UNIVERSITY, IRVINE

"Most Lutheran authors manage only a few sentences on joy. Matt devotes a whole book to the topic! St. Paul lists joy next to love in his account of the fruit of the Spirit. Christianity began with the message from an angel: 'I bring you good news of great joy!' Thus joy is one of the key elements in Christian life. Why do people so often lack it? The source of true joy is death to self and life in Christ. Obedience and joy may seem incompatible. However, the ways of inner life are often surprising. This book will inspire readers to discover joy in every part of their daily lives."

JANIS VANAGS
ARCHBISHOP OF RIGA, LATVIA

"I really love *A Little Book on Joy* as it is creative and well-written. This book had me captivated from beginning to the end. It is funny, insightful, educational, scriptural and devotional. It has a thought-provoking message on joy covering every aspect of human life. I commend this book to all pastors and lay people, theological educators and students who wish to understand what joy means and how to apply it in Christian living."

RT. REV. DR. SOLOMON RAJAH
BISHOP—EVANGELICAL LUTHERAN CHURCH IN MALAYSIA

"In *A Little Book on Joy*, Matt Harrison speaks the Gospel to the core of the postmodern Japanese mind. People today do not look for the meaning and the purpose of life any more because they are tired of an artificial, self-manipulative, goal-driven life in a depressing world. Matt Harrison presents what we need to know—that is, the joy that is given from the outside and above and moves us from the inside like a living fountain of power."

REV. DR. MAKITO MASAKI
KOBE LUTHERAN THEOLOGICAL SEMINARY

"Rare and precious, joy proves itself more than "fun" and cannot be confined to the category of our amusements. These days it seems hard for us to come by, we who are in such sore need of it. With his 'little book,' Matthew Harrison does us a big service as he defines, locates and elucidates joy, contemplating its manifold facets. This reflective work catches the reader up and carries him along with its readability and accomplished style, demonstrating its usefulness page after page. I would guess that just about everyone can find something in this book that speaks to his or her particular needs and situation in life. My recommendation for *A Little Book on Joy*? Get it, read it, and pass it on to someone who is longing for a little bit of joy—the sooner the better."

BISHOP EM. DR. JOBST SCHÖNE
INDEPENDENT EVANGELICAL LUTHERAN CHURCH IN GERMANY (S.E.L.K.)

"This is not some dry treatise. Matthew gives us a glimpse into an actual Christian's life of joy. This joyful life in Christ does not boast in itself, but it does not hide either. Joy is shared. Sadness and poverty are all around us in Madagascar. Still, God's kingdom is joy. The Gospel blesses us spiritually, and it also blesses every gift of this physical life so that we can share our joy and be a joyful blessing to others in need. This little book will help many to live joyously in God's kingdom now, and with Christ forever. 'Rejoice because your names are written in heaven' (Luke 10:20)."

REV. PROF. DAVID RAKOTONIRINA
SEMINARY PRESIDENT—STPL ATSIMONIAVOKO
ANTSIRABE, MADAGASCAR

"'Joy,' wrote C. S. Lewis, 'is the serious business of heaven.' By often side-splitting personal anecdote and through his deft probing of Holy Scripture and the Great Tradition, Matthew Harrison shows how God brings heaven's business to us here and now in Christ. Splendid!"

REV. THOMAS V. AADLAND
FORMER PRESIDING PASTOR OF
THE AMERICAN ASSOCIATION OF LUTHERAN CHURCHES
INSTRUCTOR IN SYSTEMATIC THEOLOGY
MATONGO LUTHERAN THEOLOGICAL COLLEGE, KENYA

A Little Book on JOY

The Secret of
LIVING A GOOD NEWS LIFE
in a Bad News World

Matthew C. Harrison

Illustrated by Kurt D. Onken
Study Questions by John T. Pless

CONCORDIA PUBLISHING HOUSE • SAINT LOUIS

Published 2011 by Concordia Publishing House
3558 S. Jefferson Ave., St. Louis, MO 63118-3968
1-800-325-3040 • www.cph.org

Manufactured in the United States of America

Library of Congress Cataloging-in-Publication Data

Harrison, Matthew C.
  A little book on joy : the secret of living a good news life in a bad news world
/ Matthew C. Harrison ; illustrated by Kurt D. Onken ; study questions by John
T. Pless.
     p. cm.
  ISBN 978-0-7586-3115-2
1. Joy—Biblical teaching. 2. Joy—Religious aspects—Christianity—Textbooks.
I. Title.
  BS2545.J6H37 2011
  234'.13—dc22
                              2011015143

4 5 6 7 8 9 10   20 19 18 17 16 15 14 13 12

To Kathy,
Matthew, and Markie

Contents

The Great Ninety Days of Joy after Joy

*Daily Texts with Prayers to Gladden the Heart
from Ash Wednesday through Pentecost (or any time)*

A PRELUDE TO
THIS ODE TO JOY
By John Nunes

"To my exuberant surprise, I found joy everywhere" (page 3), Matthew C. Harrison exclaims after excavating the texts. What's he been reading? Almost everything: he covers ancient authorities, Reformation leaders, as well as contemporary Christian commentators. On a journey from Augustine to Dostoyevsky, from Dr. Luther to C. S. Lewis, from Nairobi, Kenya to northern Canada, joy sparkles on every page. If an ode is a song, then this book is sung not to joy, but ultimately to Jesus (Hebrews 12:1–3).

With fearless snapshots of his own life, Harrison has penned a liberating look at just how seriously he takes this One who is truth, but not himself—nor anyone else who's straitjacketed by self-important standards of pomposity or cultural severity. Both the window-breaking, BB-gun incident (chapter 9) and his wife's forgotten birthday, leading to his faking of nausea to escape church in order to get birthday supplies (chapter 18), left me literally in tears as I reread them aloud to friends. These stories reveal a life suffused in a larger eudaemonic narrative.

Run-of-the-mill emotionalism will not do; instead, what's here is durable and enduring—centered in Christ, born from God's heart, revealed through Scripture, inspired by the Holy Spirit, grounded in the Lutheran Confessions, received in the Church, perfecting in trials, practiced in marriage and community, realized now in part, with an eye turned toward what's ultimately to come forever.

Martin Luther describes the Creator's original intent for all people: "Adam had been created in such a way that he was, so to speak, drunk with joy towards God, and rejoiced also in all other creatures" (Weimar Ausgabe 42:71). In his sobering, poetic reflection on humankind's catastrophe, the Fall into sin, Derek Walcott describes Adam's reality, post-Eden, as possessing now a "joy that was difficult, / but was, at least, his own" ["After Eden" in *Collected Poems, 1948–1984* (Farrar, Straus and Giroux, 1998), 300–301]. Harrison invites us into the triune Poet's gift of joy, fully recreated in Jesus' death and resurrection, the epicenter of Christian faith: joy that actually is not ours, but a gift coming from the Lord. We, who veer naturally toward the shadows of gloom, how do we access, in this life, such coruscating joy?

No joy worthy of God's name can be like hitting the "play" button on a Disney DVD whenever we need a high-definition, happy soundtrack. There "is no forcing it, no coercing it, no measuring it, no cooking it up" (page 8). The trek Harrison takes us on possesses no quick steps, no self-help remedies, no instantaneous fixes or superficial solutions. With practical, substantive, prayer suggestions, reflective questions, and ponder-worthy insights, we are offered Scripture's nurturing that grows the fruit of the Spirit. (See, most explicitly, "The Great Ninety Days of Joy after Joy" at the end of the book). Directed to the Means of Grace, the gate of heaven, the Word and Sacraments, Harrison calls us to confess Christ with intrepidity; but thankfully, he does so without a hint of rigidity: "So Lutheranism always has and always will recognize the very broad freedom in worship ... [but] freedom bereft of love ends in self-centeredness" (page 86).

Finally, we are escorted toward that which is beyond ourselves, that which is most expansive, the unending festival of rejoicing. Tugged along eschatologically, "through trial and cross," God's purposes unfold with grace for believers as the Holy Spirit kindles faith, inviting cold, hard, and sad hearts to "join the ever-rising crescendo of joy" (page 107) over God's new creation. That's the gift of *A Little Book on Joy*. I accept it with gratitude.

There are some modernists and others who conceive as antithetical the relationship between traditions committed to biblical and confessional orthodoxy and the outward expression of joyfulness. Harrison represents a return to that more timeless, reconciled tradition of truth, refusing to be boxed into such false dichotomies. In an article titled, "The Orthodox Imperative" the Fordham professor and Jesuit priest, Avery Cardinal Dulles (1918–2008), nails it: "Orthodoxy would have a brilliant future if it were represented with a more cheerful face" [*First Things* 165 (August/September 2006):35].

Joy?

At first, the prospect of writing *A Little Book on Joy* presented me with no joy at all. Yet I was offered the suggestion by a dear friend in Christ, who has been for me such a source of deep consolation, encouragement, and joy that I could not rid my mind of the topic. His friendship, good counsel, and guileless speaking of God's Word to me have so strengthened me in faith, hope, and love that I could not put his suggestion out of my mind, try as I might. Joy was troubling me. Despairing of my ability to duck his joyous advice, I heard the apostolic words reverberating ever more loudly in my mind, *"Rejoice in the Lord always, again I say, rejoice"* (Philippians 4:4).

I have searched through the inspired Scriptures shaking loose every available shred of information on topics such as cross and suffering, faith and mercy, but joy? Really?! Would a serious and sober Christian really concentrate on joy? Is it a topic worthy of thought in its own right? Isn't it merely a byproduct of faith in Jesus? Isn't joy something which simply arises of its own accord out of knowing the Gospel of free forgiveness in Jesus? Shouldn't I rather concentrate on grace, faith, or justification, or baptism, or the Lord's Supper, or vocation? Would a little book on joy simply amount to something like writing on flavor instead of writing a cook book? Or perhaps on the fruit instead of the tree? Wouldn't it be like an excursus on smoke instead of a manual on barbecuing? Isn't joy a subject more like the froth on the beer than the brew itself? And, worst of all, wouldn't it all be "suffocatingly subjective" (C.S. Lewis, *Surprised by Joy: The Shape of My Early Life*)? I was reminded by another dear friend of the words of a respected theologian: "Some of the most depressing sermons I've ever heard have been harangues on joyfulness." And I, after all, was certainly not going to be *harangued* into joy, much less did I wish to impose joy upon any one else! Nevertheless, disarmed and hardly exuberant, I resolved to look at the Bible.

"So many churches, so many pastors and Christians have so little joy today," my friend observed. "These are difficult times."

With the help of memory and concordances, I began inspecting the texts. Soon I was racing through the pages, Genesis to Revelation. I felt no harangue at all. It was all gift and joy over the gifts. All the while, the words of my friends bounced about my brain like a pinball. And the more texts I encountered, the longer the ball stayed in play. One part of me wished to see the happy little chrome ball slip into the pocket of despair—joy presumed, assumed, consumed, subsumed and entombed. Game over, I could simply walk away from the table, back into the world of my less joyous undisturbed prejudices.

"So many churches, so many pastors and Christians have so little joy today," my friend observed. "These are difficult times." I knew he was on to something, but I didn't know exactly what. I raced through the Psalms and found joy and rejoicing everywhere, even in the penitential psalms. I found joy in the Old Testament, in Moses, in the Prophets, in the books by Solomon. I found joy after resounding joy in Isaiah and Zephaniah. I found joy in the Gospels. I found joy on the lips of Jesus and in the lives of those whom he touched, again and again and again. I found joy on the lips of Mary and Zechariah, in the womb of Elisabeth, on the lips of angels. I found joy at the manger. I found joy at the resurrection. I found joy over life, joy in the midst of death, joy in worship. I found joy in persecution and suffering. I found Paul's letters packed with joy and rejoicing. I found joy in references to faith and hope and love. I found joy over the simplest gifts of friends, work, family, food, children and marriage. Stranger still to me was that, as I contemplated these texts in rapid fire, one after another, I, even I, began (dare I admit it?) to rejoice. I found myself *surprised*, encouraged and even delighted by joy in Christ. And wonder of wonders, I found in the Bible reference after reference to the Lord's joy over me—"More rejoicing in heaven over one sinner [a.k.a. crusty Lutheran] who repents" of his aversion to joy.

Then I turned to Martin Luther's sermons, and to the writings of C. F. W. Walther, Augustine, and the ancient fathers. Surely I could find some stodgy Lutheran or church father to temper my joy over joy. I read Athanasius, Ambrose, and the Martyrdom of Polycarp. I turned to the old Lutheran scholars and plowed through their ponderous Latin and German, like a coon dog following a fresh scent, sure to *tree* joy at any moment. I yelped with delight, and more loudly each time I found a new text, a new twist, a joyous new take on joy. I looked to Chesterton, Elert, Sasse, Gritsch, and many other modern writers. To my exuberant surprise, I found joy everywhere. What began as a spark in my smoldering understanding now broke into a flame, stoked by each new discovery. It wasn't froth. It was a deep *dunkel* draught of delight. Over a few days of the Christmas break, the pile of old tomes and concordances, Greek dictionaries and encyclopedias, sermon books and devotionals, vellum volumes and paperbacks, grew and grew to harrowing heights, encircling my easy chair.

In disgorging this introduction I feel something like Ebenezer Scrooge on Christmas morning. I've found joy, and I want to share it with you. Neck fully extended above the mountain of books encamped around me at this very moment, a dumbfounded look of happiness on my face, eyebrows at full height, mouth pursed with a cockeyed, Grinch-like frown turned to grin, unshaven and hair disheveled, I have something to say: *"Fear not, for behold, I bring you good news of a great joy that will be for all the people. For unto you is born this day in the city of David a Savior, who is Christ the Lord"* (Luke 2:10-11). Rejoice!

Turns out I've had joy after joy over joy. It's time for *A Little Book on Joy* after all.

We need this joy now more than ever. The world needs it, and Christendom needs it. If ever this joyful news was necessary for the world, then [it is] in our century of great wars and mass death. But how should we, servants of the Gospel, announce this joy to the world if we ourselves do not have it? What is missing in the churches of Christendom today is the measure of joy which the old church possessed. We all stand in great danger of having the fearful seriousness of our time, the concerns in the church and in the parsonage, even the concerns about the church which are commanded to us, not allow the great joy to arise, or kill it. This is especially true of those among us who work in "dead" congregations, who perhaps must preach in empty churches, and upon whom too much work has been placed. But it is true there, too, where the congregations are rich, sometimes too rich, where the ecclesiastical life seems to bloom and the Christian faith is in no way attacked from the outside. There it is worldly joy, the secularized substitute for the true joy of the Gospel, which threatens to destroy Christ's joy.

HERMANN SASSE, *THE CHURCH'S TIME OF REJOICING*

Joy's Perspective

1

For ye shall go out with joy, and be led forth with peace: the mountains and the hills shall break forth before you into singing. ISAIAH 55:12 (KJV)

ONE SECRET OF LIVING A GOOD NEWS LIFE in a bad news world is, in some large measure, a matter of perspective . . . somewhere between head in the clouds and feet in the mud.

The dull voice abruptly broke the monotony of a monotonous flight. We would soon encounter the chaotic bustle of the Nairobi airport. I had lost track of time since leaving Johannesburg. But instead of the usual droning ("We'll be arriving at our destination three hours late . . . Sorry for the inconvenience . . . So just sit back, relax and enjoy the remainder of this interminable flight in this rickety pile of riveted aluminum . . ."), the pilot surprised us all. "Folks I'm going to dip the right wing of the aircraft so you can enjoy a rare sight." As the plane listed, I was surprised then immediately mesmerized by joy at one of the most spectacular sites I've ever beheld. It was like a white ice mountain in a sea of billowing cotton. There, some 20,000 feet below, was the enormous snow covered crater of Mount Kilimanjaro. It was miles wide, glistening and piercing majestically and proudly through a thick blanket of East African cloud cover. I felt dwarfed by its sheer grandeur, even thousands of feet overhead. Would I ever see such a spectacular sight again in my life?

A year or two later the sun shone brightly across the Savanna on the road from Nairobi to Mombasa on the Kenyan coast. The first half of the drive is a rare Kenyan pleasure. The road is in quite good repair. The roads overall are so bad in Kenya the residents joke that "only the drunks drive straight." The windows were all down, keeping the temperature in the vehicle at a low, slow sweat. The occasional baboon attracted our faint attention. As I tried to doze, my head bounced to the right. I half-opened my eyes and scanned the horizon to the south. I had never seen it from the ground but

"One should be warned to push aside reason and heresy because they always want to count and measure things." —MARTIN LUTHER

recognized the mountain immediately. I bolted upright, surprised by the sheer joy of the spectacle. Rising alone on the horizon, not a cloud in the sky, there it was again: Kilimanjaro! And what a surprise! *"For ye shall go out with joy . . . the mountains and the hills shall break forth before you into singing."* I had no idea that we'd see it on this trip. We must have been fifty miles north of the mountain. Its breadth was overwhelming. It bothers the Kenyans to this day that Queen Victoria should have had the audacity to give what was not hers to her relative, the German Kaiser, thus forever favoring Tanzania and denying Kenya of her greatest natural wonder.

On the return, we decided to drive deep into and through Maasai country to trek up the mountain itself. Visibility was considerably lessened by a low pressure system. We hoped the clouds would clear, but it was not to be so. One of the grandest peaks in the world would not reveal herself. I had seen her greatest majesty, her gleaming white crater, without even intending to do so. Inspection without expectation. I had beheld her grandeur from foothill to highest snow covered crag, quite without any merit or worthiness in me. Now I desired to see her up close, and for the first time had actually acted to do so. But she lay impenetrably hidden. We drove onward as the plain ascended. We ascended onto the very mountain itself, only to be thwarted. The clouds lay low and heavy all about, spitting rain at us intermittently, as if laughing us to scorn. All I remember is the dirt road, the rain and mud, and thick forest and rickety villages. As darkness loomed, the end of the day beckoned us north. I was disappointed, yes; but I'd been on the mountain itself. And because I had beheld the mountain in its starkest beauty, the rain dampened, but hardly snuffed out, my smoldering joy. I was singing nonetheless.

So it is with joy, at least joy as a gift of the Spirit. There's no forcing it, no coercing it, no measuring it, no cooking it up. Whenever that happens, joy quickly is faked and feigned and, in fact, extinguished. "One should be warned to push aside reason and heresy because they always want to count and measure things." (Luther, Festival Sermons 1:137) There's no calculating when and precisely how it will strike or when it will be felt and to what extent. I am certainly not going to offer the reader anything like a "Joy-O-Meter" in this little book, or "Ten Sure-fire Ways to Put Joy into Your Life." Nonetheless, where there is Jesus, there is joy . . . and a lot of it in the Bible. There is joy in the most profound truth of God's Word (the Gospel of Christ) and the simplest grandeur of the tiniest particle of creation. But joy at its best is like the kingdom of God; it "comes by itself without our prayer" (Small Catechism, 2nd Petition).

We ourselves have no constant or even enduring view from, or into, the heavens in this life. But we are given a fabulous glimpse into heaven itself in the Bible. When the clouds break and the heavenly rays reveal the peaks, we behold joy. And there is an attitude of joy in life which can and does encompass it all, even in the face of severe trial or death. "Even Job on his dunghill was not deserted by the Lord" (Ambrose, *Ancient Christian Commentary on Scripture,* 6:296). In fact, there is a kind of joy so profound, so enduring, that it can only be known and felt in one way. Its weaker shadows must be completely dashed and lost. Here's the secret: if we seek joy for its own sake, we will not find it. If we seek Jesus, we shall be engulfed and inundated by joy, and quite by surprise.

"Even Job on his dunghill was not deserted by the Lord."

—AMBROSE

The Bible is a book about Jesus; more than that, the Bible actually delivers Jesus to us in divine words which are "living and active, sharper than any two-edged sword" (Hebrews 4:12). It is more than possible for us to "live a Good News life in a bad news world"; it's God's great pleasure and desire for us to do so. But if it is to be a life which knows true joy, it shall be a joy in perspective. The Bible occasionally dips a wing for us, and we see beams of beatific-heavenly joy, something like seeing Kilimanjaro from 20,000 feet. Once in a while we'll get the picture of the whole, or as much of the whole as can be seen at once from earth. But most of the time we'll view life from the perspective of a trek in the mud, or as ants atop a dunghill. By faith we know the mountain's there, and by the same faith we may share its joy.

More than anything, I'd like this little book to be a bit of "joy in the mud" for the reader—a little book on the perspectives of joy I have found along the way, much to my great surprise and delight, muddy feet and all.

Study Questions:

Read or sing: "Dear Christians, One and all, Rejoice" (*LSB* 556).

1. In Galatians 5:22, Paul identifies "joy" as a fruit of the Spirit. How does this text confirm Pastor Harrison's statement that "there's no forcing it, no coercing it, no measuring it, no cooking it up"?
2. How is joy like the kingdom of God itself?
3. How does God give us joy? See Luke 2:1-11. Where do you hear this message today?
4. C. S. Lewis authored a book, *Surprised by Joy*. How does Jesus surprise us with joy?
5. Where does God give us "joy in the mud"?

Something to Think About:

"Why is there so little of holiday and joy—so little of daring and praise and enthusiasm in our Christianity? Because there is so little of faithfulness, so little of faith in our calling."

EINAR BILLING, *OUR CALLING* (FORTRESS, 1964), 44

The Father's Joy

2

And he arose and came to his father. But while he was still a long way off, his father saw him and felt compassion, and ran and embraced him and kissed him. And the son said to him, "Father, I have sinned against heaven and before you. I am no longer worthy to be called your son." But the father said to his servants, "Bring quickly the best robe, and put it on him, and put a ring on his hand, and shoes on his feet. And bring the fattened calf and kill it, and let us eat and celebrate. For this my son was dead, and is alive again; he was lost, and is found." And they began to celebrate. LUKE 15:20-24

The text might be rendered more dynamically: "And running, the father almost bowled over his son, bear-hugged him for joy, and kissed him over and over again." Before the son had managed a word of penance, the father turned and shouted! "He's home! Let's celebrate. Prepare the feast!" That's who the Father is. Jesus could hardly have illustrated more concretely the contrast between the religion of his Father and that of the Pharisees who were grumbling at him. "This man receives sinners and eats with them" (Luke 15:2). The cornerstone of Pharisaic religion was "joy through compliance." There is no running father in Pharisaism. They meant well. The disobedience of their fathers and mothers brought captivity and occupation to Israel, and they were determined to comply with the law to every "jot and tittle" and beyond.

But they were so certain of their self-chosen path to restoration that they preferred the cold embrace and kiss of the Law to the joyous embrace of the Father of mercies, and Joy Incarnate in Jesus—the God who runs to embrace sinners. They preferred sacrifice to mercy. Compliance religion of the Law finally ends in a narrow, smug, twisted, and self-absorbed "joy" in no one but the self and its self-chosen strictures. By contrast, the religion of the Lord broadens things, beginning with the human heart. "I will run the way of thy commandments, when thou shalt enlarge my heart" (Psalm 119:32; KJV). The father does not run in the religion of the Law. In the religion of Jesus, he sprints!

Compliance religion of the Law finally ends in a narrow, smug, twisted, and self-absorbed "joy" in no one but the self and its self-chosen strictures. By contrast, the religion of the Lord broadens things, beginning with the human heart.

I was just a boy. Our life was simple, our house small, our family inauspicious. But Mom and Dad never failed to find ways to add a little fun to life. One Christmas, Dad brought home a snowmobile to two boys, gazing, mouths agape out the front window. It was only minutes later that my brother and I were dressed for the weather and climbing about this sleek machine, itching for the first shot at it. It was a brilliant move for the family. Every weekend or holiday when snow prevailed in Northwest Iowa, we'd haul the machine out to Cousin Larry's farm and spend the afternoon together. Dad would pull us via rope on an old truck tire inner tube over snow-covered hill and dale. We'd try to hang on, only to lose the battle higgledy-piggledy in a tumble of arms, legs, snow and laughter. I can see in my mind's eye my dad on that machine, one knee kneeling on the seat (as he liked to ride), head held high above the windshield, grinning ear to ear, glasses fogged, circling to give us another go at it. "Do it again, Dad! Again!"

We rarely get enough of what we don't need to make us happy. The prodigal son, nearing the end of his joy ride, realized he had become just one joyless pig among others.

My little sister, who to this day retains something of her unique combination of timidity and total self-confidence, had decided it was time for her to solo on the snow machine. Dad cautiously consented, offered the requisite instruction and warnings. He pointed her in a safe direction. My brother and I braced for the boredom, reduced to making snow angels. Little Sis took her first spin at the speed of a glacier, tediously consuming our treasured minutes of icy rough and tumble racing and daring.

As she pulled away Dad watched her traverse every snow-covered inch. I noticed him growing anxious as Sister increased to moderate speed and headed in the direction of a barbed wire fence at the edge of the property. Concerned for her safety he cupped his hands, and began to shout her name, warning her away from the fence, already leaning and stepping toward her. Then (and I shall never forget it because it is the only time I'd ever seen my father run flat out) fearing for her safety he took off at full speed, shouting her name. Of all my childhood memories, this one stands forever uniquely etched upon the palette of my mind. I saw my father in dark, green coveralls, gloves, and snow boots, running as fast as he could over an uneven fallow field, through a foot of snow, anxiously screaming my sister's name. I was face to face with the depth of love of a father for his child. And I know to this day, that this man, so very understated, in many ways so un-animated, is animated by an incomprehensively deep love for my mom, my sister, my brother, and me—and for Jesus. And it has always given me profound joy to realize it and recall it. As if his running angst were itself a prayer, my sister—completely oblivious to her father's snow-muffled shouts—was gently carried out of danger.

We rarely get enough of what we don't need to make us happy. The prodigal son, nearing the end of his joy ride, realized he had become just one joyless pig among others. At long last he longed for what he had despised, and despised what he had so longed for. His feet had "run to evil" (Proverbs 1:16), convinced it would be the nectar of joy. Now he trudged back to plead mercy that he might find the place of a disobedient hireling, more than he deserved. The table was turned. While he rejoiced in the world, his father was in misery. When he returned in misery, his father rejoiced with exceeding joy. Day by day, hoping against hope, praying the son would remember his love, the father waited. Finally, his son returned from despair to the embrace of joy on the very path which had taken him from joy to the arms of despair.

> "He giveth power to the faint; and to them that have no might he increaseth strength. Even the youths shall faint and be weary, and the young men shall utterly fall: But they that wait upon the Lord shall renew their strength; they shall mount up with wings as eagles; they shall run, and not be weary" (Isaiah 40:29-31).

Youth fainted utterly. The father waited. In a moment, strength renewed, he ran to his beloved, wayward, prodigal. There are many accounts in the Bible of saints running at the joy of seeing Jesus. Zachaeus "ran ahead and climbed a sycamore tree to see him" (Luke 19:3). "Peter rose and ran to the tomb" (Luke 24:12). The women "departed quickly from the tomb with fear and great joy, and ran to tell his disciples" (Matthew 28:8). There are also accounts of false saints running with pseudo-joy. The demoniac, "when he saw Jesus from afar, ran and fell down before him" (Mark 5:6). Even the rich young man ran to Jesus to pose his horrid, gospel-denying question: "A man ran up and knelt before him and asked him, 'Good Teacher, what must I do to inherit eternal life?'" (Mark 10:17).

But Jesus' parable of the prodigal son provides the grandest sprint ever recorded. It unveils for us the heart of God the Father in Christ. Our God rejoices over sinners and sprints to show it. That's the secret to a good news life after wallowing in a bad news world.

He will rejoice over you with gladness (Zephaniah 3:17). All these things signify that their consciences would experience that fatherly sweetness of the kingdom of the Lord. The sense is this: "You will feel joy. You will feel in your conscience that the Lord is kindly disposed toward you, that he surely is a kind Father to you in all things." You see, the Lord is said to rejoice over us when he causes us to sense his favor. . . . He has expressed the nature of the kingdom of Christ very aptly and emphatically. For thus it happens for the righteous that he allows them to be attacked . . . in various ways, and to be troubled by many evils, so that they be conformed to their King. Yet he adds that feeling of joy, that security of heart, so that all things may become sweeter, so that nothing can separate them from the love of God, Romans 8:39.

—MARTIN LUTHER, *LUTHER'S WORKS,* 18:361

THE FATHER'S JOY :: 17

Study Questions:

Read or sing: "Thanks to Thee, O Christ, Victorious" (*LSB* 548).

1. Helmut Thielicke called the parable of Luke 15:11–32, "the parable of the waiting father." After carefully re-reading the parable, note how the father's waiting issues forth in joy.
2. "The cornerstone of Pharisaic religion was 'joy through compliance.'" Where was the Pharisees' joy located?
3. How had the prodigal son ended his "joy ride"? See Proverbs 1:16.
4. Read Isaiah 40:29–31. How is this Old Testament prophecy descriptive of the prodigal son?
5. Note Martin Luther's comment on Zephaniah 3:17. How does Luther picture joy experienced in the human conscience? What is the Gospel foundation for this joy?

Something to Think About:

"Wherever forgiveness is proclaimed there is joy and festive garments. . . . God is so completely different from what we thought or feared. News that he has sent his Son to us and is inviting us to share is an unspeakable joy."

HELMUT THIELICKE, *THE WAITING FATHER* (HARPER, 1959), 29

The Greeting about Jesus: Rejoice!

3

And the angel came in unto her, and said, Hail [Rejoice!], thou that art highly favored, the Lord is with thee: blessed art thou among women. And when she saw him, she was troubled at his saying, and cast in her mind what manner of salutation this should be. And the angel said unto her, Fear not, Mary. LUKE 1:28-30 (KJV)

And as they went to tell his disciples, behold, Jesus met them, saying, All hail [Rejoice!]. And they came and held him by the feet, and worshiped him. Then said Jesus unto them, Be not afraid: go tell my brethren that they go into Galilee, and there shall they see me. MATTHEW 28:9-10 (KJV)

From his conception to his resurrection, the divine greeting "Hail!" or "Greetings!" and "Don't be afraid!" stand like enormous pillars of joy compassing the thirty-three years of Jesus' life and ministry in ancient Israel. But "what manner of salutation should this be?" (Luke 1:29, KJV). The little Greek word *chaire* is translated variously as "Greetings!" (ESV) or "Hail!" (KJV). The same word is used by St. Paul to say, "Rejoice in the Lord!" (Philippians 3:1). So in the annunciation to Mary the angel greeted her saying, "Rejoice!" In other words, "These very words I'm speaking are great Gospel Good News for you!" And when Jesus appeared risen from the dead to his disciples, he said to them, "Rejoice!" He had risen. They knew it by their very grasp on his feet. They hardly needed any command to rejoice. With his presence, his joyous "Rejoice!" swooped among them and accomplished its own demand—something like what happens when in the name of Jesus we say, "Grace! Mercy and Peace!" The word and everything packed into it, effects the very thing it says; so also and especially the divine greeting, "Rejoice!"

What's more, of some 326 occurrences of words used for "joy" in the New Testament, the most common cognates for joy (*chara*, "inner joy," and *chairein*, "to rejoice") are derived from the same root *char-* as in the Greek word for "grace," *charis*. There is a very close connection between the two concepts [*Dictionary of Paul and His Letters* (InterVarsity Press, 1993), 511].

Imagine that! Grace and joy have "a very close connection"! So Jesus' life in Galilee is grace incarnate, inaugurated and capped by (what else?): "Rejoice! Don't be afraid! God's free favor (grace) is yours!" Mary and the astonished post-resurrection disciples in both instances were fearful. But surprised by joy, they were comforted by grace and given the gift of rejoicing.

My friend, John Pless, tells the story of an unforgettable greeting on a dark night in Hyderabad. Of the many countries I've visited over the past decade or so, India stands in a class (caste?) by itself. It is as confusing as it is intriguing, as disturbing as it is delightful. The maze of lane-less streets, choked with endless tangled lines of traffic, cars, buses, vans, tri-shaws, motorcycles, bicycles, ox-carts and pedestrians, isn't confusing at all, compared to the enigmatic difficulty of navigating the interminable intersections and cul-de-sacs of caste and race.

John landed at the Hyderabad airport late at night to be greeted by two men holding a sign bearing his name. They spoke virtually no English. Soon John was treated to a harrowing ride in a motorcycle sidecar in Indian urban traffic, knowing little of whence he came and nothing of where he was going. I've had more than enough similar experiences to know that not knowing one's destination, or the duration of the trip, or where one is to sleep, at the end of thirty-six hours in trains, planes and airports, doesn't add much to the glamour of cross-cultural travel. Finally the cycle arrived at its goal, a rooming house.

John made his way behind an unknown guide in a dark and unknown building to an even darker hall. The door was opened into a room still darker. His rooming house host left as John groped to arrange his things and quickly get to bed. "Confusion may remain for a night, but I can figure out where I am in the morning," he thought. Both John and I have been in circumstances where a lone,

So Jesus' life in Galilee is grace incarnate, inaugurated and capped by (what else?): "Rejoice! Don't be afraid! God's free favor (grace) is yours!"

twenty-five-watt bulb and the pulse of a few amps of electricity sent rodents scurrying along baseboards for the cover of cracks and crevices in old structures which had already been old before their time. The mind flashes with odd thoughts at such moments: "Did I get that plague vaccination?"

Suddenly a stir in the dark sent a bolt of trepidation up his spine. He was not alone in the room. *Gnguu-uuulp!* The hair standing up on the back of his neck proved it. As his eyes adjusted to the dimmest of light, the lump in a bed across the small room turned toward him. The bed creaked. In a millisecond John "cast in his mind what manner of greeting this might be." Just as his adrenal gland spiked to render his exhausted carcass fit for fight or flight, he heard a familiar Australian voice say, "John? That you, mate?" Adrenalin, laughter, and joy immediately erupted as two old friends John Kleinig and John Pless, each far from home, met on a dark night in Hyderabad, quite by surprise. Both had come to teach in an Indian Lutheran seminary. Neither had any idea exactly when they might stumble upon each other. Both were surprised and delighted by a joyous greeting. All anxiety was at an end as fear and unease turned to joy and much needed rest.

On a moonlit night in Jerusalem, hell faked a joyous greeting. "Hail!" "Greetings, Rabbi!" The devil masquerades as circumstance requires. He'll allure with the kiss of a prostitute in the dark: "In the black and dark night ... there met him a woman with the attire of a harlot.... So she caught him, and kissed him" (Proverbs 7:9 ff.). Or he'll piously abhor the kiss of a prostitute in the light. "This man, if he were a prophet, would have known who and what manner of woman this is that toucheth him: for she is a sinner" (Luke 7:39). If we're bedeviled, we will do anything but stare at ourselves in the mirror and see ourselves for what we are. There is always someone to greet with feigned joy and secret derision when we don't believe either in Jesus or our own sinfulness.

Judas betrayed him with feigned joy: "Hail! (*chaire*) Rabbi!" (Matthew 26:49). The betrayer knew the psalm, "Kiss the Son, lest he be angry" (Psalm 2:12). But even then, Jesus was not angry with him. "Friend, do what you came to do." Soon the deceptive greeting of a traitor gave way to the twisted, joyfully-mocked "Hail, King!" of professional henchmen.

> And they stripped him, and put on him a scarlet robe. And when they had platted a crown of thorns, they put it upon his head, and a reed in his right hand; and they bowed the knee before him, and mocked him, saying, Hail (*chaire*), King of the Jews! And they spit upon him, and took the reed, and smote him on the head (Matthew 27:28–30 KJV).

Most people who read or hear the Bible happily identify with Mary, the shepherds, Elisabeth, or maybe even John the Baptist. Because we all have our moments, we may identify with Peter. We love to hate the Pharisees and scribes. We despise Judas, Herod, Pilate, and the soldiers who mocked and beat Jesus. Perhaps when feeling particularly sanctified, we'll admit we can't believe the disciples could be such dolts. Looking at the Bible this way amounts

If we're bedeviled, we will do anything but stare at ourselves in the mirror and see ourselves for what we are. There is always someone to greet with feigned joy and secret derision when we don't believe either in Jesus or our own sinfulness.

to an inoculation. In all of this, there's not much of the threat of an outbreak of joy. None of it dares to come face to face with the real depths and perversity of sin, my sin. None of it stares Judas in the face and beholds itself in full, unalloyed, naked, sinful truth. None of it looks in the mirror and says,

> The saying is trustworthy and deserving of full acceptance, that Christ Jesus came into the world to save sinners, of whom I am the foremost. But I received mercy for this reason, that in me, as the foremost, Jesus Christ might display his perfect patience as an example to those who were to believe in him for eternal life" (1 Timothy 1:15–16).

The secret of living a good news life in a bad news world is to see myself, my sins, my darkest thoughts, my constant failings and weaknesses in the dark characters and their darker moments in the Bible. "We do not want joy and anger to neutralize each other and produce a surly contentment; we want a fiercer delight and a fiercer discontent" (Chesterton, Orthodoxy). Then I shall have the joyous revelation of Martin Luther that "Christ dwells only in sinners"

(*Luther's Works*, 48:13), and I'd better be careful to actually be one. Only real sinners need a real Savior. Despairing of myself, all the joyous greetings of Jesus are mine.

> And, lo, the angel of the Lord came upon them, and the glory of the Lord shone round about them: and they were sore afraid. And the angel said unto them, Fear not: for, behold, I bring you good tidings of great joy, which shall be to all people. For unto you is born this day in the city of David a Savior, which is Christ the Lord.
>
> LUKE 2:9–11

Study Questions:

Read or sing: "Rejoice, Rejoice, Believers" (*LSB* 515).

1. Read Luke 1:28–30 and Matthew 28:9–10. How does the Lord's joy dispel and displace fear?
2. How are joy and grace related in the New Testament?
3. How did Judas feign joy in Matthew 25:49–50? How was Jesus mocked with words of joy in Matthew 27:29–30? The Holy Scriptures hold up Judas and the soldiers that we might see ourselves in them. Read 1 Timothy 1:15–16. How does this passage restore us to the joy of salvation?
4. Comment on this statement from G. K. Chesterton: "We do not want joy and anger to neutralize each other and produce a surly contentment; we want a fiercer delight and a fiercer discontent."
5. How does Luke 2:9–11 illuminate Luther's bold declaration that "Christ dwells only in sinners." In light of this, discuss Pastor Harrison's observation that "Only real sinners need a real Savior."

Something to Think About:

"For He has purchased and won me from all sins, from death, and from the power of the devil, not with gold or silver, but with His Holy, Precious Blood . . .' The measure of my joy at being thus delivered is determined by the extent to which I am aware of the heinousness of my sin, the awful finality of death, and the baleful intention of the ancient foe of souls."

ARTHUR CARL PIEPKORN [*UNA SANCTA* 7:1 (ADVENT 1946)]

The Joy of the Holy Spirit: A "Joy Set Before"

4

Let us run with endurance the race that is set before us, looking to Jesus, the founder and perfecter of our faith, who for the joy that was set before him endured the cross, despising the shame, and is seated at the right hand of the throne of God. HEBREWS 12:1-2

The secret to living a good news life in a bad news world is the joyous knowledge—by the gracious enlightenment of the Holy Spirit—that Christians are not always happy and joyous. Far from it.

Now that may seem an odd statement, to be sure, particularly in *A Little Book on Joy*. But some of the most miserable people I've known have been tormented by the belief that they must always demonstrate the joy of the Holy Spirit to others, particularly to demonstrate to themselves and others that they've "got the Holy Ghost." It's all meant in the best way. But it ends in one of two spiritual death traps. It can force a Christian into either hypocrisy or deep despair. It may even lead to a bizarre and lethal combination of the two. Hypocrisy renders us "whitewashed tombs" (Matthew 23:27). It makes us pretend to be what we know deep down we aren't. But we continue demanding what we aren't, of others! Despair takes the law seriously, but stupidly and arrogantly thinks its two-bit sins are worth more than the blood of God in flesh, which paid for the sins of the world. Pastors are particularly susceptible in this regard because they are to "be examples to the flock" (1 Peter 5:3), yet at the same time they face deep spiritual struggles and failings, just like James, John, John Mark, Barnabas, Peter, Apollos, and Paul. "Oh wretched man that I am!" (Romans 7:24).

Jeremy—I'll call him Jeremy—was tormented by an extreme form of this spiritual schizophrenia. He had gone out of his way to introduce himself to me and was truly interested in finding some support in his walk with Christ. His disability rendered him terribly lonely and depressed, and his religion wasn't helping things. And I bothered him. When he asked when I had "given my life to Christ" I said, "I was baptized as an infant. I was raised by Christian parents, and I don't ever recall a time when I did not believe that Jesus died for my sins. I think the main thing is that Jesus gave his heart to me." Jeremy was kind, but suspicious.

When he asked when I had "given my life to Christ" I said, "I was baptized as an infant. I was raised by Christian parents, and I don't ever recall a time when I did not believe that Jesus died for my sins. I think the main thing is that Jesus gave his heart to me." Jeremy was kind, but suspicious.

For the next year or two we would meet, sporadically. He shared his testimony. Even as I write these very lines, I'm filled again with the tensions I always felt in his presence. He was a deeply humble person (in fact, so humble it ended up being a vice for him). Over time he shared some of his deep spiritual struggles and questions with me. But I often felt as though he were trying to disciple me into a "real experience of the Holy Spirit," as he put it. I was always guarded. In retrospect, all these years later, I don't think that's really so much what he was trying to do. He just didn't know any other way of being a Christian. And truth be told, I think his truthfulness about not living up to the Law bothered me deeply because

I knew the Law condemned me, too, as Jeremy spoke of his own struggles. Perhaps I was too worried about discipling him—being the pastor after all!—than simply befriending him in Christ. I find joy in knowing God can occasionally speak through an ass, as he has been known to do (Numbers 22:28).

Once on a walk on a country road Jeremy again revealed his despair. He did not know if he really was a Christian because he was talking the talk but not walking the walk. Christianity was to be full of joy, but he felt none of it. I remember turning to this poor tormented man, whom I'd invited to church many times. (He could not stand to be in crowds.) "Look, Jeremy, do you believe you are a sinner?" "Yes," he replied. "Do you believe that Jesus is the Son of God who died on the cross for your sins?" "Yes, I do," he replied, "but I'm just not walking the walk." I responded, "Jeremy, nobody can follow the Law as God demands. The very fact that you are so troubled about being a Christian is proof that in fact you have the Holy Spirit and are a Christian! If the Holy Spirit weren't alive and kicking in you, you wouldn't be troubled about this issue! Jesus came for sinners. For Pete's sake, Jesus died for sinners! Come join us sinners at church!" He never did. I lost track of him years ago.

Joy is pervasive in the Bible, to be sure. Joy is the fruit of faith (Galatians 5:22). Faith's content is simply Jesus. Just like good works are the fruit of faith, so is joy. Where there's an apple tree, there are apples . . . but in due season. Out on the Harrison farm, my grandmother tended and pruned what she called her "Wintertime Greenie" apple tree. But oh, it seemed an eternity before those huge, delicious, sour apples would be in full harvest come late summer. Joy, too, has its seasons.

It should give you the greatest comfort and joy that the Bible is filled not only with evidence of joy, but also of times of no joy. And that does not mean the Holy Spirit is absent.

For everything there is a season, and a time for every matter under heaven:

> a time to be born, and a time to die . . .
> a time to weep, and a time to laugh;
> a time to mourn, and a time to dance (Ecclesiastes 3:2, 4).

Job, if he is anything, is honest to God. That's a gift of the Spirit! The Psalms bear witness to the full range of human emotion, and plenty of it is anything but joy, e.g., Psalm 42. And it's all inspired by the Holy Spirit! The Prophets struggled (think of Jeremiah) with the gamut of human foibles and frustrations, including their own. James counted them "happy" only after the fact. "Take, my brethren, the prophets . . . for an example of suffering affliction, and of patience. Behold, we count them happy which endure" (James 5:10–11). But the greatest example for the fact that there are times and seasons of joy in the Christian life is Jesus himself, "the author and perfecter of our faith, who for the joy that was set before him, endured the cross" (Hebrews 12:2).

Jesus is the very offspring or fruit of the Holy Spirit. He is God the Son, filled with the Spirit of God by nature. The Spirit descended upon him in the form of a dove to begin his public ministry. "This is my Son whom I love!" the Father spoke from heaven (Matthew 3:17). He lived a full and human life, with the range of human thoughts, feelings and emotion, but all without sin. We have them all too, yet with sin. But that doesn't mean that the feelings we have—so far as Jesus himself had them—are necessarily sinful in and of themselves. Thus it's by no means sinful not to feel joy in life "out of season."

As a baby, Jesus cried and was hungry. Later he was tempted (Matthew 4:1). He was tired (Mark 6:31). He wept (John 11:35). He was angry (Matthew 21:12; 23:1ff.). He was frustrated with his disciples on many occasions (Matthew 16:23; 17:17). He was deeply "troubled" (Mark 14:33). He was "annoyed" that little children were prevented from seeing him (Mark 10:14). He mourned and felt compassion (Luke 7:13). He was sad and mourned when

John the Baptizer was murdered (Matthew 14:13). He was disappointed by nine lepers who failed to return (Luke 17:17). He felt dishonor and pain over his own family (Matthew 13:57). He felt rejection (Matthew 21:42). He anguished over Jerusalem (Matthew 23:37). He had angst over people seeking his death (Matthew 26:1ff.). He experienced betrayal (Matthew 26:24). He was sorrowful "even to the point of death" (Matthew 26:38). He felt disappointment (Matthew. 26:40ff.). He felt deserted (Matthew 26:56). He felt indignant over false accusations (Matthew 26:57ff.). He felt pain (Matthew 26:67). He felt sorrow over ridicule and insult (Matthew 27:29). He felt the abandonment of the Father (Matthew 27:46). He felt death (Matthew 27:50).

The very fact that you are so troubled about being a Christian is proof that in fact you have the Holy Spirit and are a Christian! If the Holy Spirit weren't alive and kicking in you, you wouldn't be troubled about this issue!

Some old Lutheran theologians defined joy as an affect or emotion; a sort of happiness over a past event remembered, a present happy reality experienced, or a future happiness expected. Jesus looked to the Word of God regarding the future, and it sustained him in the joyless present. "Let us run with endurance the race that is set before us, looking to Jesus, the founder and perfecter of our faith, who for the joy that was set before him endured the cross, despising the shame, and is seated at the right hand of the throne of God" (Hebrews 12:1–2). Moments such as the Transfiguration or his baptism—"This is my beloved Son!"—were joyous past events, were remembered by Jesus (and actually grabbed hold of him!) during the joyless times. And these events are the same for us because in our baptism the Lord speaks the same Word to us: Beloved!

One must read all of Psalm 22 to comprehend what Jesus was thinking on the cross. "My God, My God, why have you forsaken me?" was spoken in the pit of joyless hell, abandonment by God. And yet in the misery, the future joy of what he had done was contemplated and believed, though hardly experienced. "They shall come, and shall declare his righteousness unto a people that shall be born, that he hath done this" (Psalm 22:31).

It gives me the greatest joy to know that Christians, while filled with the Holy Spirit, are not always filled with the greatest joy, or joy at all. Far from it. The joy of the Spirit is often a "joy set before." That's the secret to living a good news life in a bad news world.

Paul himself exclaims (Romans 7:24): "Wretched man that I am! Who will deliver me from this body of death?" He accuses his "body," which he really should have loved, and gives it a very ugly name, calling it his "death," as though he were saying: "My body afflicts and harasses me more than death itself." Even in his case this interrupted the joy of the Spirit. He did not always have pleasant and happy thoughts about his future inheritance in heaven, but over and over he experienced sadness of the spirit and fear.

—MARTIN LUTHER, *LUTHER'S WORKS*, 26:393

Study Questions:

Read or sing: "Why Should Cross and Trial Grieve Me" (*LSB* 756).

1. What is the "secret to living a good news life in a bad news world"?
2. How would you distinguish happiness from joy?
3. Read Hebrews 12:1–2. How does this text anchor us in genuine joy?
4. What are the "two spiritual death traps" that capture those who wrongly think that they must always demonstrate the joy of the Spirit? How does the Holy Scripture guard us against this danger?
5. What can we learn from the story of Jeremy?
6. Does the absence of joy mean the absence of the Holy Spirit? Defend your answer scripturally.
7. Read James 5:10–11. What is the connection between endurance in times of affliction and joy?
8. Review the listing of emotions experienced by Jesus in this chapter. Do we experience any emotions not experienced by our Lord?
9. How is joy past, present and future?
10. Read Psalm 22. What does this psalm tell us about joy in the suffering and exaltation of the Messiah?
11. Read carefully the citation from Luther. What do we learn about the Christian's joy from Luther's testimony?

Something to Think About:

"Then the church's time of waiting will be over, then the end of the time of faith will have come; then joy will no longer be veiled in fear and holding back; then will come the time of fulfillment, the time of everlasting seeing, when blessing breaks in."

DIETRICH BONHOEFFER, "ASCENSION DAY SERMON 1933," *DBW* 12:471

The Joy of Repentance:
A Joy without Compare

5

Don't waste any time denying your sins.

—MARTIN LUTHER, *THE HOUSE POSTILS*, 3:140

We measure things. We learn how to live and cope by measuring things. From our earliest days of cognition we learn by comparison. We attempt to measure ourselves against others and others against ourselves. As children we are bigger or smaller, taller or shorter, louder or softer. As life marches on, it's faster or slower, smarter or not so smart, cooler or nerdier. Sooner than we expected, the comparisons are for better or worse, for richer or poorer, having children sooner or later, houses larger or smaller, and cars newer or older. Then it's heavier or thinner, tax brackets higher or lower. Finally it's more grey or less grey, blood pressure higher or lower, cholesterol normal or above normal, stronger or weaker, a fifty-fifty chance of making it through the surgery, etc. We measure and compare virtually every aspect of our lives against others. It's more than natural to do so.

Both the Law and the Gospel defy all measurement and therefore defy the kind of comparisons we are so hardwired to make. That's why the Gospel can't be compared to other news. It can't be believed but by the power of the Holy Spirit. The secret of living a good news life in a bad news world is realizing that real joy is a joy without comparison. Christ releases us from comparison and measurement at the most crucial nexus of our lives—the point where Christ lays hold of us, gives us joy, and makes us his for eternity. The Law renders its judgment: total condemnation. The Gospel renders a judgment too: total righteousness. David illustrates this principle.

David is the consummate saint-sinner in the Bible. War hero, king, kingly prefigurement of Christ, and inspired writer of psalms, he nevertheless fell into a tawdry web of sex, lies, and murder. His evening stroll on the roof and glance at Bathsheba bathing sent him into a spiral which nearly cost him eternity, but, ironically, has been an eternal blessing to us in the texts David left behind.

Christ releases us from comparison and measurement at the most crucial nexus of our lives—the point where Christ lays hold of us, gives us joy, and makes us his for eternity.

Did the king walk on his roof because he suspected he might see what he saw? And why was Bathsheba in view of the king anyway? The questions are unanswered by the text, but the answers are easily inferred. There's an old saying: "Give the devil the tip of your finger, and soon he'll have the whole arm." David looked. He stared. He asked who she was. He sought her. He committed adultery with her. She became pregnant. Her husband was at war. David devised a plan to cover his tracks. He called her husband Uriah home from the front, but the honorable man wouldn't sleep with his wife while his men were in the field. David got him drunk and tried again. Even alcohol couldn't break Uriah's honor. The sexual obsession and the cover-up grew to murderous proportions. Uriah, the Hittite convert, was more honorable, by far, than the Lord's very own prophet and king. In fact, there was no comparison. Uriah was a man of faith and acted like it. David was not and acted accordingly. David delivered Uriah's death warrant by the honorable man's own hand to general Joab, who executed him with a military maneuver. "Put him at the front of the line, and have the army back away from him so he's sure to die." Cover-up. Abuse of power. Murder. David sacrificed the profound joy of the Lord for moments of fleeting pleasure, and then for long years of internal agony and public shame.

There is infinite joy in "fearing, loving and trusting in God above all things" (Small Catechism, First Commandment). But David feared being exposed a sinner, loved his lust, and trusted in his own machinations.

There is joy in the name of the Lord. But the king and prophet of God "lied and deceived by his name" and failed to "call upon it in every trouble, pray, praise and give thanks" (Small Catechism, Second Commandment).

There is joy in "preaching and his word." But for the better part of a year, David did not, would not, could not "gladly hear and learn it" (Small Catechism, Third Commandment).

There is joy in the respect and recognition of blessing in offices "and other authorities" placed by God. But David despised and abused his high office, abused and despised the offices of Uriah and Joab, and did anything but "love and cherish them" (Small Catechism, Fourth Commandment).

There is joy in "helping and supporting our neighbor in every physical need" (Small Catechism, Fifth Commandment). David premeditated an honorable man's murder.

There is joy in "leading a sexually pure and decent life in what we say and do" (Small Catechism, Sixth Commandment). But David's lust and lack of contentment with what the Lord had given led him from lust to cold-blooded murder.

There is joy in helping our neighbor retain his "money or possessions" (Small Catechism, Seventh Commandment). But David took Bathsheba and Uriah's very life—all "his money and possessions"—in a consummately "dishonest way."

There is joy in speaking what is true about our neighbor, not in "telling lies about" him or "betraying him" (Small Catechism, Eighth Commandment). But David sacrificed joy on the altar of the worship of the father of lies.

There is joy in "helping and being of service" (Small Catechism, Ninth Commandment) to our neighbor in keeping his inheritance and house. But David got everything which was Uriah's in a way he had hoped would at least "only appear right."

There is joy in being content with what we have and "not enticing or forcing away our neighbor's spouse . . . and urging them to stay and do their duty" (Small Catechism, Tenth Commandment). But David's discontent, covetousness, and lust destroyed his neighbor's life and his own.

No matter how rotten a scoundrel I may be, I can always find someone on a lower rung. "I've done some horrible things in my life, but I wouldn't do that!"

There is great joy in keeping these commandments: "Therefore we should also love and trust in Him and willingly [gladly!] do what he commands" (Small Catechism, Ten Commandments, Conclusion). But gladness dies along with the demise of repentance and faith. "The thing that David had done displeased the LORD. And the LORD sent Nathan to David" (2 Samuel 11:27–12:1).

There were rumors of David's deed flying all about the king's court, but rumors always hover around power and money. David was keeping up righteous appearances, the mirage of a faith absent, like gold papered over a rotted, termite-riddled beam. He had to, so he believed; otherwise his enemies would bring him down. By comparison with his former, faithful self, nothing appeared so radically different about David's life, at least from afar. Nathan made a brilliant move to save the hypocrite king, and Jerusalem with him. (See how Psalm 51 ends!)

No matter how rotten a scoundrel I may be, I can always find someone on a lower rung. "I've done some horrible things in my life, but I wouldn't do that!" Witness the ranking of prison inmates with respect to offenses committed, particularly those against children. But that's merely an extreme case of what we all suffer: self-justification by comparison. There is always someone else who deserves hell, or deserves it more than we do anyway. Nathan had the task of speaking the Law to David so that he would be condemned, and condemn himself. That is the only path to joy.

> "There were two men in a certain city . . . The rich man had very many flocks and herds, but the poor man had nothing but one little ewe lamb, which he had bought. And he brought it up, and it grew up with him and with his children. It used to eat of his morsel and drink from his cup and lie in his arms, and it was like a daughter to him. Now there came a traveler to the rich man, and he was unwilling to take one of his own flock or herd to prepare for the guest who had come to him, but he took the poor man's lamb and prepared it for the man who had come to him." Then David's anger was greatly kindled against the man, and he said to Nathan, "As the LORD lives, the man who has done this deserves to die, and he shall restore the lamb fourfold, because he did this thing, and because he had no pity." Nathan said to David, "You are the man!" (2 Samuel 12:1–7)

Finally, David spoke the truth: "David said to Nathan, 'I have sinned against the LORD.' And Nathan said to David, 'The LORD also has put away your sin; you shall not die'" (2 Samuel 12:13). The consequences of David's duplicity were heavy, but the path to joy was open, if painful, and David was back on it. "Make me to hear joy and gladness; that the bones which thou hast broken may rejoice. Hide thy face from my sins, and blot out all mine iniquities" (Psalm 51:8–9 KJV).

You have surely noticed that when you find yourself at odds with family, friends, fellow church members, you quickly sum up the situation, absolve yourself, or at least judge yourself to be of lesser guilt by comparison. "But he/she acted like a fool, not me!" "Do you suppose, O man—you who judge those who do such things and yet do them yourself—that you will escape the judgment of God?" (Romans 2:3). David profoundly illustrates what is true of all of us. It is very easy to measure the "speck" in our neighbor's eye, and ignore the "log" in our own (Matthew 7:3). Our sins may not be as spectacular as David's, but the tenfold condemnation of the Law fully applies to each of us. The path to true joy has no detour in the road around the Law of the Lord. The Law brings repentance, and the path to joy is via our own *via dolorosa* (path of sorrows). If the Law has not produced total self-condemnation, there can be—will be—no joy. Instead, there will be only self-righteousness and hypocrisy, salted with an arrogant condemnation of and snooping for the sins of others—a bad conscience seared into numb bitterness by denial. What a horrid, joyless way to live by comparison. We are all guilty of it.

"Don't waste any time denying your sins." Christ is waiting on the other side with a good conscience and a joy without compare.

To the chief Musician, A Psalm of David, when Nathan the prophet came unto him, after he had gone in to Bathsheba.

Have mercy upon me, O God, according to thy loving kindness: according unto the multitude of thy tender mercies blot out my transgressions. Wash me thoroughly from mine iniquity, and cleanse me from my sin. For I acknowledge my transgressions: and my sin is ever before me. Against thee, thee only, have I sinned, and done this evil in thy sight: that thou mightest be justified when thou speakest, and be clear when thou judgest. Behold, I was shapen in iniquity; and in sin did my mother conceive me. Behold, thou desirest truth in the inward parts: and in the hidden part thou shalt make me to know wisdom.

Purge me with hyssop, and I shall be clean: wash me, and I shall be whiter than snow. Make me to hear joy and gladness; that the bones which thou hast broken may rejoice. Hide thy face from my sins, and blot out all mine iniquities. Create in me a clean heart, O God; and renew a right spirit within me. Cast me not away from thy presence; and take not thy holy spirit from me. Restore unto me the joy of thy salvation; and uphold me with thy free spirit. Then will I teach transgressors thy ways; and sinners shall be converted unto thee.

Deliver me from bloodguiltiness, O God, thou God of my salvation: and my tongue shall sing aloud of thy righteousness. O Lord, open thou my lips; and my mouth shall shew forth thy praise. For thou desirest not sacrifice; else would I give it: thou delightest not in burnt offering. The sacrifices of God are a broken spirit: a broken and a contrite heart, O God, thou wilt not despise. Do good in thy good pleasure unto Zion: build thou the walls of Jerusalem. Then shalt thou be pleased with the sacrifices of righteousness, with burnt offering and whole burnt offering: then shall they offer bullocks upon thine altar. Psalm 51 (KJV)

"Joy implies psalm singing, confession laments for sins; the combination of the two molds the wholly perfect Christian. . . . What is sweeter or more wholesome than praise of God and constant self-condemnation?"

CASSIODORUS ON PSALM 42:5
ANCIENT CHRISTIAN COMMENTARY ON SCRIPTURE, 7:330

Study Questions:

Read or sing: "Baptismal Waters Cover Me" (*LSB* 616).

1. Read 1 John 1:10. In light of this text, comment on Luther's statement: "Don't waste any time denying your sins."
2. How does the Law drive us to measurement? How does the Gospel defy measurement?
3. Read 2 Samuel 11:1–12:15. How does this story from the life of David illustrate the dynamics of sin, repentance, and faith?
4. How does David violate each of the Ten Commandments?
5. How does the Lord's absolution on the lips of Nathan change David's life? Also see Psalm 51:8–9.

Something to Think About:

"May our dear Lord Jesus Christ show you his hands and his side and gladden your heart with his love, and may you behold and hear him only until you find your joy in him. Amen."

MARTIN LUTHER, LETTER OF APRIL 30, 1531
TO BARBARA LISSKIRCHEN WHO SUFFERED FROM ANXIETY
LETTERS OF SPIRITUAL COUNSEL (WESTMINSTER, 1955), 117

A Just Joy

6

God shows his love for us in that while we were still sinners, Christ died for us. Since, therefore, we have now been justified by his blood, much more shall we be saved by him from the wrath of God. For if while we were enemies we were reconciled to God by the death of his Son, much more, now that we are reconciled, shall we be saved by his life. More than that, we also rejoice in God through our Lord Jesus Christ, through whom we have now received reconciliation. ROMANS 5:8-11

"I didn't come to kill you." He was an imposing figure. He had an even more imposing reputation. But what he had been known for, well-earned to be sure, was not why I remember him. He had become an ever more devout Missouri Synod Lutheran and regularly shared the good news of Jesus with, and invited to church, people who wouldn't have given him the time of day had he not been who he had been. This former purveyor of intimidation had become an ambassador of reconciliation. This fact was all the more significant because it was not readily apparent. He was so unassuming, even with his rather imposing stature, that no one who hadn't come to know him would be aware of his past. Same man, same haunts, same circle of people—but for an ever-deepening, transformative joy of being justified in Christ.

Another man in a nearby community had sinned egregiously

against my friend and his family. The former "intimidator" went directly to the man in question, to his very doorstep in fact. The guilty party opened the door and began frantically to plead (with good reason), "Don't kill me! Don't kill me!" My friend responded, "I didn't come to kill you. I came to forgive you." He wasn't on a mission of retribution. He was on a mission of reconciliation. *"If your neighbor sins against you, go and tell him his fault, between you and him alone"* (Matthew 18:15). He hadn't come to exact justice. He had come as one justified sinner seeking the repentance of and reconciliation with another sinner. The flesh relishes the thought of retribution. The spirit rejoices in reconciliation.

The righteousness of Christ credited by faith is transformative. It reckons us what we are not and cannot be in and of ourselves—per-

The righteousness of Christ credited by faith is transformative. It reckons us what we are not and cannot be in and of ourselves—perfectly righteous with the righteousness of Jesus.

fectly righteous with the righteousness of Jesus. We are reckoned "just." Then, like a good tree planted, it produces more and more fruit (Matthew 7:17), especially joy, and makes us evermore what we have been freely declared to be—righteous in Christ. Declared forgiven, we cannot but be forgiving. But let's back up.

St. Paul says that this righteousness was obtained fully by Christ's cross—*"we have now been justified by his blood."* What has been achieved, obtained, and perfected by Christ outside of us, before us, and without us (two thousand years ago on a cross and via a resurrection), is delivered to us and reckoned to us in the word of the Gospel. Because it's already accomplished, it can't be achieved by doing anything. The deed is done. That's why Jesus' last words were, "It is finished" (John 19:30). The benefits of Christ's death and resurrection are received, laid hold of, by faith. Faith simply lays hold of the gift, and even the faith, which receives the gift, is itself all gift. So St. Paul wrote, *"For by grace you have been saved through faith. And this is not your own doing; it is the gift of God, not a result of works, so that no one may boast"* (Ephesians 2:8–9). Reconciliation occurred in Christ's death—"God was in Christ reconciling the world unto himself" (2 Corinthians 5:19)—and this same reconciliation is "received" here and now. And it's powerful. In fact, it is the most powerful force for joy in the world.

This central teaching of the Bible is a profound mystery and a profound key to a joyous life. *"He who knew no sin became sin for us that we might become the righteousness of God"* (2 Corinthians 5:19). Think of it. The Bible calls Christ "sin." God in the flesh is called "sin." And just as amazing, by virtue of Christ, we are called "the righteousness of God." When God looks at us, he sees only the perfect life, death, and resurrection of Jesus.

> Every Christian may rejoice and glory in Christ's birth as much as if he had himself been born of Mary as was Christ. How is it possible for man to hear of greater joy than that Christ has been given to him as his own? (Martin Luther, *Church Postils*, Lenker ed., 1:144, 149).

Reconciliation occurred in Christ's death—"God was in Christ reconciling the world until himself" (2 Corinthians 5:19)—and this same reconciliation is "received" here and now. And it's powerful. In fact, it is the most powerful force for joy in the world.

St. Paul says that the kingdom of God is a matter "of righteousness and peace and joy in the Holy Spirit" (Romans 14:17). Where Christ's righteousness is laid hold of, there is peace of conscience, and where there is peace of conscience, there is a profound joy. The word for "joy" used by Paul here is *chara*—that deep, inner, spiritual joy . . . a joy that abides midst all the turmoil and anxieties of life.

When we confront God, he says to us, "I didn't come to kill you. I came to forgive you." *"For God did not send his Son into the world to condemn the world, but in order the world might be saved through him"* (John 3:17). Equipped with such joy, a "just joy," we find ourselves freed to act as God himself with our neighbor. "I didn't come to kill you. I came to forgive you." Joy! *"We also rejoice in God through our Lord Jesus Christ, through whom we have now received reconciliation"* (Romans 5:11).

Study Questions:

Read or sing: "Alleluia! Let Praises Ring" (*LSB* 822).

1. Read Romans 5:8–11. How is "the righteousness of Christ credited by faith transformative"?
2. Pastor Harrison writes "the flesh relishes the thought of retribution. The spirit rejoices in reconciliation." How is this reconciliation expressed in daily life?
3. How was reconciliation with God achieved? How is it received? See John 19:30, Ephesians 2:8–9, and 2 Corinthians 5:19.
4. Christ's righteousness is our justification. How does Luther describe the depth of this joy?
5. How does "I didn't come to kill you. I came to forgive you" echo the message of John 3:17?

Something to Think About:

"It is not enough to believe that Christ is risen from the dead, because neither peace nor joy, power nor might follow, but I must believe that the resurrection happened for me, so that I might delight that my own sin and death are overcome there. This is true faith."

MARTIN LUTHER, "SERMON ON THE FIRST SUNDAY AFTER EASTER ON JOHN 20:19FF.," PREACHED ON APRIL 10, 1523, *LUTHER'S WORKS* 69:334

A Community of Joy

7

If one member suffers, all suffer together; if one member is honored, all rejoice together. 1 CORINTHIANS 12:26

Once a man said to me, "Pastor, I wouldn't join that church of yours for anything. They're all a bunch of hypocrites!" I responded, "True. And there's always room for one more."

Quite despite itself, its weaknesses, its shortcomings, its mistakes and sins (and in many ways precisely because of such things), the Church is a community of joy. The secret to living a good news life in a bad news world is learning both to lay down our burdens upon Christ and the gathered community (the Church), and, in turn, to take up the burdens of others gathered there. Luther stated it brilliantly.

> Whoever is in despair, distressed by a sin-stricken conscience or terrified by death or carrying some other burden upon his heart, if he would be rid of them all, let him go joyfully to the sacrament of the altar and lay down his woe in the midst of the community and seek help from the entire company of the spiritual body—just as a citizen whose property has suffered damage or misfortune at the hands of his enemies makes complaint to his town council and fellow citizens and asks them

for help. The immeasurable grace and mercy of God are given us in this sacrament to the end that we might put from us all misery and tribulation *[Anfechtung]* and lay it upon the community, and especially on Christ. Then we may with joy find strength and comfort . . . (*Luther's Works*, 35:53).

There's always room for another sinner in church. It's true that "no man is an island," and doubly true that we are not meant as Christians to face this life alone. That's because the Church is a body, the "body of Christ," as the New Testament repeatedly affirms (Ephesians 4:1ff.). The Word of God comes from outside of us. Christ acted and continues to act outside of us, for us. The Word of God confronts us with a reality quite at odds with anything we might stir up within ourselves.

"Since therefore the children share in flesh and blood, he himself likewise partook of the same things, that through death he might destroy the one who has the power of death, that is, the devil, and deliver all those who through fear of death were subject to lifelong slavery" (Hebrews 2:14–15). Christ's Incarnation and Passion are the ultimate "communal events." He took on the flesh of all humankind, the ultimate participation in the lives of others. Even when faith comes by an individual reading the text of the Scriptures, such faith is not the result of an individual's self-chosen interaction with a document which conveys historic events. The text of the Scriptures puts us face to face with a person, Jesus Christ, the very Word of God (John 1:1). To confront the Bible is to confront Christ. *"The word of God is living and active, sharper than any two edged sword, piercing to the division of soul and of spirit, of joint and of marrow, and discerning the thoughts and intentions of the heart. And no creature is hidden from his sight, but all are naked and exposed to the eyes of him to whom we must give account"* (Hebrews 4:12–13). Encountering Jesus is at the same time the pull toward his body. That body is a community of

believers, who gather locally to receive his gifts continually in the word of the Gospel preached by one called by the community, to be absolved, and to receive his body and blood.

One of the many ways the New Testament reveals this truth is by using compound words that include the preposition "with" (in Greek, *syn-*). These words are almost always plural.

It's true that "no man is an island," and doubly true that we are not meant as Christians to face this life alone. That's because the Church is a body, the "body of Christ," as the New Testament repeatedly affirms . . .

"We were *buried together with* Christ in baptism . . ." (Romans 6:4).

"We have *died together with* Christ . . . and we believe we shall also *rise together with* him . . ." (Romans 6:5–6).

"We are *fellow heirs with* Christ, and if we have suffered together with him, we shall also be *glorified together with* him" (Romans 8:17).

"Having been *buried together with* him in baptism, in which you were also *raised with* him . . ." (Colossians 2:12).

"You have been *made alive together with* him . . ." (Colossians 2:13).

So it's no surprise that joy is also found in the plural. The word "they rejoiced together" is found three times in Luke's Gospel. Elisabeth's friends and relatives "rejoice together" with her at the birth of John the Baptizer (Luke 1:58). When the lost sheep and the lost coin are found, the friends and neighbors are invited to "rejoice together" (Luke 15:6; 15:9).

In his profound discussion on the Lord's Supper and its ramifications (making us one body), St. Paul elaborates. *"For just as the body is one and has many members . . . so it is with Christ. For we have all been baptized by the one spirit into one body"* (1 Corinthians 12:12). As members of one body, Christ, the members of the Church have lives intertwined by and with Christ. *"You are one body of Christ and with many members. If one members suffers, all suffer together with it. If the one member is glorified, all rejoice together with the one member"* (1 Corinthians 12:26). The Church is a community of joy because in it we both share our sufferings (universal because of sin and weakness), and we rejoice with and for one another.

I recall an event which took all of about eight seconds, and it illustrates how the Church lives this corporate life. It didn't happen in the Church, but it has direct application. On more than one occasion, I've laughed out loud traveling past the stadium in Sioux Falls, South Dakota. But I've never written about why.

Sioux City (Iowa) East High had nearly finished the 1979–80 football season, undefeated and ranked number one in the state. (The older I get, the better I was.) We were well into our final regular season game, playing Sioux Falls (South Dakota) Lincoln High on their home field, Howard Wood Stadium. The number one teams of South Dakota and Iowa, respectively, both known for powerhouse offenses, were locked in a defensive battle. Well into the third quarter, neither team had scored. We failed to convert on yet another series and had to punt, again. It was getting tense. The conference championship was riding on the game, as well as our playoff placement.

As the team's center and long-snapper, I must admit, hiking the ball twelve yards to the punter was a task I did not relish (though I also ended up doing it in college while pursuing my major: football). Having both arms, neck, and head thrown upside-down between your legs, with all the force you can muster, is not the optimal position from which to "block" (i.e., defend yourself against the assaults of a defensive nose tackle (or worse, some rabid middle linebacker) whose sole fourth-down goal in life was to make the center's life miserable on such occasions. (The rules have since changed.) Well, I don't recall what got into me, but something went horribly wrong. I knew it the split second the ball left my hands.

I vividly recall that fraction of a second, peering through my legs at the inverted vision of the punter leaping into the air, one hand extended as far as possible to field the snap. It was no use. It wasn't even close. The ball flew at least ten feet over his outstretched arm. My attention reverted to my immediate nose tackle problem as I heard the defense scream with banshee delight. A golden opportunity unfolded in milliseconds before them. The crowd gasped, cringed and screamed for delight (though opposing sides in differing order) within a few seconds. But for a set of better than average sphincter muscles, my stomach would have been dropped at the forty yard line.

As the team's center and long-snapper, I must admit, hiking the ball twelve yards to the punter was a task I did not relish . . .

I stayed with the nose tackle briefly, then turned to see the punter and quarterback, Bob Larson, scramble back, pick up the ball, dodge a tackle or two, and proceed to throw a pass to our tight end who, had run an impromptu pattern. Miraculously, the pass was caught for a first down. A few more plays, and we managed to score, but failing on the extra point. We went on to win the game 6-0.

As long as I live, I'll never forget the scream of the head football coach, Terry Stevens, through his clenched teeth, the muscles in his head, jaw, and neck so tight that *"H-A-R-R-I-S-O-N!!!"* echoed from his pursed lips with tremolo and saliva as the offense ran to the sidelines. He never said another word. He didn't have to.

I learned something. The fault had been all mine—*all mine,* as was more than obvious to everyone. The team quickly adjusted, altered the plan, and acted on instinct. They not only compensated for my error, they turned it into an opportunity for joy. That was a *great* team. As a husband, a father, a pastor, a churchman, I often "snap it high," and great folks around me cover and even turn my mistakes for good. And perhaps even more importantly, when others "snap," often egregiously so, I find myself thinking about how I've been in the same boat, or easily could be and will be, and I'm ready to scramble and cover others' weaknesses. That's what it is to live mercifully and the secret to living joyously in the community of the church and family, amidst the mishaps and mistakes of life.

Bonhoeffer depicts the Church, our community of joy, in a much more compelling way.

> As Christ bore with us and accepted us as sinners, so we in his community may bear with sinners and accept them into the community of Jesus Christ through the forgiveness of sins. We may suffer the sins of one another; we do not need to judge. That is grace for Christians. For what sin ever occurs in the community that does not lead Christians to examine themselves and condemn themselves for their own lack of faithfulness in prayer and in intercession, for their lack of service to one another in mutual admonition and comforting, indeed, for their own personal sin and lack of spiritual discipline by which they have harmed themselves, the community and one another? Because each individual's sin burdens the whole community and indicts it, the community of faith rejoices amid all the pain afflicted on it by the sin of the other and, in spite of the burdens placed on it, rejoices in being deemed worthy of bearing with and forgiving sin. "Behold, you bear with them all and likewise all of them bear with you, and all things are in common, both the good and the bad" (Luther). [Bonhoeffer, *Life Together* (Fortress, 2005), 102]

Study Questions:

Read or sing: "Lord Jesus Christ, the Church's Head" (*LSB* 647).

1. What does 1 Corinthians 12:26 tell us about the communal nature of joy?
2. How does Luther describe the community in bearing the burdens of the individual believer?
3. What does the New Testament's use of the preposition "with" teach us about life in Christ? See Romans 6:4; 6:6–7; 8:17; Colossians 2:12–13?
4. Read Luke 1:58; 15:6; 15:9. How do these texts illustrate that joy is to be shared?
5. Read 1 Corinthians 12:21–26. How does Paul speak of both suffering and joy as corporate? What does this mean for the life of your congregation?
6. How does Pastor Harrison's ill-fated attempt at football illustrate the Apostle Paul's point about community?
7. Reflect on the citation from Bonhoeffer's *Life Together*. How might we apply his words to our living together in the congregation?

Something to Think About:

"For just as the Lord did not create an earth for only one man, so he did not create a heaven for just one man. There is no solitary earth and there is no solitary heaven, and he who can wish for a complete separation from all men, whether temporal or eternal, does not have the love which is of God, but rather has a dark, arrogant hatred of both God and man."

WILHELM LOEHE, *THREE BOOKS ABOUT THE CHURCH* (FORTRESS, 1969), 49.

The Joy of Marriage

8

If one member suffers, all suffer together; if one member is honored, all rejoice together. 1 CORINTHIANS 12:26

After finishing college at Seward, my wife Kathy and I served as lay missionaries in a remote Cree Indian village in Ontario, Canada. One day we decided we'd go for a snowmobile ride. I pulled the machine in front of our little shack. I glanced behind me to see Kathy hopping aboard, and I took off. I headed down the skidoo trail on the frozen lake on a bright clear, frigid day, chatting happily with my dear wife (or so I thought). I had made it nearly a half-mile before I realized that no one was talking back. Suddenly I did a hard double take and turned to see the empty seat right behind me. Looking back at the distant village, she was nowhere to be seen. Turns out I had taken off just as she straddled the seat, but before she'd sat down. Kathy stood there watching for several minutes, as I became an ever-smaller dot in the distance, wondering how long it would take me to notice. Laughing in comic disbelief, wondering just how long it would take me to notice something amiss, she finally turned around and went into the cabin to wait. We laughed about it then, and still do to this very day.

So it is with marriage. You won't get very far trying to travel alone in a relationship, talking to yourself, or at someone else. Luther noted that he would see young couples utterly infatuated with each other. They'd get married and in a year want to end it all. But like Jesus turning the water into wine at Cana, so the trials, difficulties and time turn the water into wine, and only those know how sweet it is who have tasted it (*The House Postils*, 1:237). "*Let your fountain be blessed, and rejoice in the wife of your youth . . . be intoxicated always in her love*" (Proverbs 5:18–19).

But the joy of marriage is ever more elusive. Shockingly, the divorce rate for members of the Missouri Synod is about as high as that of the general population! All too often, even among Christians, the joy of marriage fades. The intoxication of falling in love ends in a hangover of loneliness and pain. "Love at first sight is easy to understand; it's when two people have been looking at each other for a lifetime that it becomes a miracle" (Amy Bloom).

There are three simple facts that are the secret to a joyous marriage, the secret to living a good news life in a bad news world.

The first secret of joy in marriage is that it is God's own act. "*Then the Lord God said, 'It is not good that the man should be alone; I will make a helper fit for him'*" (Genesis 2:18). The ultimate crown of God's creation, woman, is made after all the animals. The Lord wanted to impress upon Adam the incomparable wonder of what he was about to do for the man. Adam had named all the animals, "*But for Adam there was not found a helper fit for him*" (Genesis 2:20). Some would balk right away, alleging that the woman as a "helper fit for him" is demeaning. But the Lord God himself is pleased to be called a "helper." *Ezer* is the Hebrew word, and the name "Eliezer" means "God is my helper" (Numbers 3:32). "Fit for him" simply means that the woman would be in the same glorious image of God—righteous, intelligent, a delightful living, eternal soul to be a "soul mate" for life. When Adam awoke from his divinely induced slumber, he discovered a rib gone and a miracle before his eyes. Genesis records the first human words. They were an expression of boundless joy over the gift he beheld: "*This at last is bone of my bones and flesh of my flesh. She shall be called Woman, because she was taken out of Man"* (Genesis 2:23). A dynamic rendering of the text might well read, "Wow! She's the one!" So it is that when a man fails to love his wife, he is also deeply confused about himself. *"In the same way husbands should love their wives as their own bodies. He who loves his wife loves himself"* (Ephesians 5:28).

Why is this a key to joy in marriage? *"A man shall leave his father and his mother and hold fast to his wife, and they shall become one flesh"* (Genesis 2:24). It all teaches the profound, divine intent of joy between husband and wife. It explains, very simply, the natural male-female attraction. But much more than this, it teaches that marriage is God's. Just as he brought Adam to Eve and Eve to Adam, he brings one spouse to the other, to this very day. Marriage is a divinely-rendered contract. God's action is primary. That's why the marriage vows quote Jesus, *"What God has joined, let no one separate"* (Matthew 19:6).

This is a life-saving, joy-saving truth. Inevitably, relationships go through highs and lows. Infatuation and emotions ebb and flow. It is necessary, crucial for a couple to recognize from the start, that no matter how I feel, no matter how we struggle, no matter how we fail each other, God put us together and wants us together. And the same God desires that we rejoice in each other. Without this mutual conviction, a marriage is doomed, and even if it endures, it's doomed to joylessness. But with it, the door is open to an enduring, growing, blossoming joy. *"I perceived that what God does endures forever"* (Ecclesiastes 3:14).

"Happy marriages begin when we marry the ones we love, and they blossom when we love the ones we marry" (Tom Mullin).

The second secret of a joyful marriage is that marriage is an act of the will. In the vows we state, "for better, for worse, for richer or poorer, in sickness and in health," "I will." Virtually every marriage goes through times when we simply don't *feel* love. I always ask couples preparing for marriage a simple question: What is love?

The response is almost invariably, "It's what you feel for another person." Well, what happens when the feeling is not there? What happens when, after an argument, or a period of poor communication, or a short night because of a sick child, or troubles with relatives, the *feeling* of love just isn't there any more? The flesh immediately looks for a different path to joy.

All too often, even among Christians, the joy of marriage fades. The intoxication of falling in love ends in a hangover of loneliness and pain.

But love, in its most fundamental form, is not, in fact, emotion. It is the will to act for the benefit of another, no matter how it feels. Paul bids husbands *"love your wife as Christ loved the church and gave himself up for her"* (Ephesians 5:25). The truth holds good for wives too. Christ acted for the benefit of all of us, quite without a continual warm fuzzy feeling of love and joy. *"My Father, if it be possible, let this cup pass from me; nevertheless, not as I will, but as you will"* (Matthew 26:39). He willed to do it. He submitted to the will of his Father as an act of love, and the result is endless joy for the world. Marriages go through emotional ups and downs. I love Joyce Brothers' quip, "My husband and I have never considered divorce . . . murder sometimes, but never divorce." Willing to love through the troubled waters is an invaluable building block for joy in a marriage. *"Two are better than one, because they have a good reward for their toil"* (Ecclesiastes 4:9).

The third secret to joy in marriage is that with the deep conviction that God has put a couple together, and that couple wills to be together—come hell or high water—the feelings of love and joy, over time, will emerge in a way more powerful and surprising than any words can possibly express. Jesus loves marriage. He provided an additional one hundred and fifty gallons of fine wine as his inaugural miracle— and that after the people had "drunk freely" (John 2:10). Jesus loves *your* marriage and promises everything you need to sustain you, even through dire times of difficulty and joylessness.

It's nice to hear from time to time that a couple has never had a disagreement, but I'm always suspicious when I hear it. Conflict between sinners is inevitable. And there is no more intimate look at another sinner, or at our own sins, than from the vantage of marriage. And conflict, while caused by sin, is not all bad. *"By sadness of face, the heart is made glad"* (Ecclesiastes 7:3). Conflict drives us toward solutions. When married couples work through conflict, their children learn that life's bumps can be endured and conquered. Conflict clears the air of irrationality and emotion and provides the opportunity to come together again and work toward resolution. It can erode our pride and stubbornness just enough for us to seek ways to find greater joy in each other. Gary Chapman's, *The Five Love Languages: How to Express Heartfelt Commitment to Your Mate* (1996), was a profound help to Kathy and me in finding greater joy in our marriage.

But love, in its most fundamental form, is not, in fact, emotion. It is the will to act for the benefit of another, no matter how it feels.

"A threefold cord [husband, wife, and Christ] is not quickly broken" (Ecclesiastes 4:12). Did you know that while one in two couples who marry today will divorce, only one in a hundred couples who are regularly in church together will split? Years ago as a young married couple, Kathy and I would have a spat about something or other. In the course of an argument our sinful defense mechanism goes into automatic. "But if you only did so and so, we wouldn't have this problem." I remember times when we would drive to

church together, not speaking because of a conflict unresolved. Right at the front of the service we'd be reminded that we are each baptized. And then came the magic moment, the breakthrough to joy again. "I, a poor, miserable sinner, confess unto You all my sins and iniquities with which I have ever offended You . . ." I knew what I was confessing. I knew she knew what she was confessing. Inevitably, our hands would find that of the other and we'd be absolved by our pastor, together. *"Weeping may remain for a night, but joy comes in the morning"* (Psalm 30:5).

Luther commented on Psalm 45:

> "We are afflicted in every way, but not crushed; perplexed, but not driven to despair; persecuted, but not forsaken; struck down, but not destroyed; always carrying in the body the death of the Lord Jesus, so that the life of Jesus may also be manifested in our bodies." So the bridesmaids [pastors] lead the church and strengthen her with the words of faith and the consolation of the Holy Spirit and encourage her: "Hold on and trust." But it is a great art to know that this is the Christians' dance, when the heart throbs because of the bitter hatred of the world, the trial of the devil and sin, as Paul complains of the "thorn and messenger of Satan" (2 Cor. 12:7). It is a hard dance and impossible for the flesh. Yet it must be done, so that we must admonish ourselves and say what someone else said: "Here do your dance" [Aesop]. The promises are the flutes, the ministers of the Word are the dancers who lead the maidens. These two can sweeten the bitter dance. For the church has no other joy than the Word (*Luther's Works*, 12:296).

Marriage is "a hard dance," but the forgiving Word of God "sweetens" it. "Over time Jesus turns the water into wine, and only those know how sweet it is who have tasted it" (Luther). *"For your love is better than wine"* (Song of Solomon 1:2). Words fail me to describe my love for my wife. She knows me intimately. She knows my deepest failings and disappointments. She knows me like no one else ever can or will. She hurts when I hurt. She rejoices when I rejoice. She wills to love me still. *"Many women have done excellently, but you surpass them all"* (Proverbs 31:29). I know her and appreciate her in ways now that are only possible because we've continued to "dance," and Jesus is still at the party turning water into wine. The Lord has made good on his promises.

I look forward with a love so profound, so emotional, and so total that I am at wit's end merely to describe it. Paul compares our life in Christ to marriage, or rather marriage to our life in Christ (Ephesians 5). Our mutual forgiveness has opened to us a panorama of God's grace that would have been impossible otherwise. It's a view of grace, which has only expanded exponentially with our family. I'm loved, and I love. Joy. Irrepressible, incomparable, unparalleled joy. *"Enjoy life with the wife whom you love"* (Ecclesiastes 9:9).

Behold, you are beautiful, my love. SONG OF SOLOMON 4:1

Study Questions:

Read or sing: "O Father, All Creating" (*LSB* 858).

1. How does the snowmobile story serve as a foil to 1 Corinthians 12:26 and also illustrate "joy" in marriage?

2. Reflect on stanza 2 of "O Father, All Creating" (*LSB* 858) and this quote from Pastor Harrison, "But like Jesus turning the water into wine at Cana, so the trials, difficulties and time turn the water into wine, and only those know how sweet it is who have tasted it." How does the Lord teach us "in testing" to know the "gift divine" of marriage?

3. Read Genesis 2:20 and Numbers 3:32. In our Christian vocation as husband or wife, how is the Lord a helper to us?
4. Read Genesis 2:21 and 1 John 5:6–8. How is the creation of Eve from Adam's side similar to the creation of the Church?
5. What is the role of the "will" in marriage? How does it assist us in finding joy in marriage?
6. Read Ecclesiastes 4:12. How is forgiveness (as a gift of Christ) the third cord of marriage?

Something to Think About:

"Now the ones who recognize the estate of marriage are those who firmly believe that God himself instituted it, brought husband and wife together, and ordained that they should beget children and care for them. For this they have God's word, Genesis 1:28, and they can be certain that he does not lie. They can therefore also be certain that the estate of marriage and everything that goes with it in the way of conduct, works, and suffering is pleasing to God. Now tell me, how can the heart have greater good, joy, and delight than in God, when one is certain that his estate, conduct, and work is pleasing to God?"

MARTIN LUTHER, *LUTHER'S WORKS* 45:38

The Joy of Family

9

Eric Gritsch provides a marvelous little comment on the joyous side of the family and home life of Martin Luther:

> Luther enjoyed good food and wine, often breaking out in song after a meal and inciting his guests to sing along—occasionally interrupted by noisy children and accompanied by the howling dog Klutz. [Eric Gritsch, *The Wit of Martin Luther* (Fortress Press, 2006), 100]

Complete with howling dog, it reminds me (and I'm sure you too) of the thousands of hours spent with family and friends around the kitchen table. My grandparents had a great oak table. I remember grandma asking the "boys" (my dad and uncles) to help put in the extra leaves as all the "kids" were arriving for Sunday dinner. It seemed to expand limitlessly, just like the potato salad. We'd eat, then we'd tell stories, laugh and giggle, play jokes on each other, and play cards and cribbage into the night.

The little story that follows has become a mainstay of joy and humor about our kitchen table.

"This is the worst week of my *li–i–i-fe!*" And it really had been. My older son had broken his hand just a few days previously. (That story is recounted in *Christ Have Mercy: How to Put Your Faith in Action*, Concordia, 2008). Soon after, another incident added insult to injury, literally.

Our family loves to stop at antique malls. Each one of us has one or two things we like to collect. I look for old bluegrass LPs (an extension of my habit of banjo playing). Kathy collects embroidered hankies. At the time of this incident, the boys were still into toy weapons.

Well, there was this Daisy BB gun. "Dad, can we get this?" Ah, nostalgia. "Boys, I had one just like it when I was a kid." It was the cowboy style lever action. A flood of positive memories inundated my mind. "Hmmm? Only eight bucks? Sure! It will be good for you boys to learn some responsibility . . . Now when I was a kid we played cowboys and Indians. In fact, I shot the neighbor kid in the leg once. Ha! I can still see Jed W. howling to high heaven, eyes shut in pain, and hopping on one foot. I'll never forget that. Hilarious . . ."

Then I caught myself, "But don't you *ever* think of shooting another person. This BB gun is *very* dangerous, and you could put an eye out in a split second. Understand?"

We three cowboys moseyed up to the counter. My wife approached (a few hankies in hand). I obfuscated, holding the gun against my opposite leg. "Find some hankies, honey? Nice." My feigned interest only resulted in suspicion.

"Mom! Look at this cool gun! It really shoots! Dad said we could get it, and we're gonna buy some BBs on the way home!"

"I don't know; that could be kind of dangerous. Matt, do you think the boys are ready for that?"

The response I give in such circumstances, and almost always live to regret it is, "Ah . . . (right hand held head high, palm facing the wife, waving dismissively downward) don't sweat it. It'll be *just fine*. Why, when I was a kid, I had one just like it. It'll be good for 'em . . ."

My wife pursed her lips and gave that slight up-and-down head nod that looks like "yes" but really means "no." It's a double affirmative, which is actually a negative. "Ya . . . right." It also automatically lodges a preliminary, though unspoken, "I told you so."

We got home, and the boys immediately headed for the back porch, the older cowboy with gun in hand, the younger toting the ammunition. The doily sheriff blocked the door.

"Matt, aren't you going to go out and supervise them?" My response, "Ah . . . (right hand held head high, palm facing wife, etc.), they'll be fine. Don't worry about it. When I was a kid, etc., etc. . . . I told them *not* to shoot toward the neighbors, and if they shoot the neighbor's window, *they'll* be paying for it." The sheriff pursed her lips, shook her head "yes" (meaning "no" or "ya, right") and relented—"I told you so," now doubly lodged.

I walked into the house, and the younger boy was on the phone with grandma who just happened to call right then. I heard this much of the conversation, "No, Mom's not mad at Matthew at all. She's mad at Dad for letting us play with the gun."

I settled into my easy chair. Not ten minutes . . . not *ten minutes* later, the little one came running back into the house! "*Matthew shot out the glass!*" "What?!!!!" I jumped out of my chair and headed for the driveway toward a loud bawl. There was the marksman, gun in hand. "This is the worst week of my *li–i–i–fe!*" The little one led me to the back of my Toyota van. The *entire* rear window was shattered, half the glass fallen out. The gun had jammed. As he tried to get it to fire again, my son pointed the barrel safely downward at the driveway. After a few attempts, it fired a BB. The shot ricocheted off the asphalt and struck the window of the van. That eight-dollar gun had just cost me $300 in less than ten minutes.

As I stood surveying the carnage, my wife came out for a look. She looked at me. She looked at the van. She looked back at me and said, "Ah . . . (right hand held head high, palm facing away with dismissive swiping motion) they'll be fine . . ."

I walked into the house, and the younger boy was on the phone with grandma who just happened to call right then. I heard this much of the conversation, "No, Mom's not mad at Matthew at all. She's mad at Dad for letting us play with the gun."

To this day the whole family laughs about the incident. Each one chimes in with his or her part in the story. The blame gets laid on Dad, and we howl with laughter together with extended family or friends. It's pure joy, at Dad's well-deserved expense.

The Gospel of free forgiveness in Christ frees us to expect mistakes, forgive them, and to find the humor in them after the fact.

St. Paul provides the prescription for joy in the family.

> Put on then, as God's chosen ones, holy and beloved, compassion, kindness, humility, meekness, and patience, bearing with one another and, if one has a complaint against another, forgiving each other, as the Lord has forgiven you, so you also must forgive. And above all else put on love, which binds everything together in perfect harmony. . . . Wives, submit to your husbands, as is fitting in the Lord. Husbands, love your wives, and do not be harsh with them. Children, obey your parents in everything, for this pleases the Lord. Fathers, do not provoke your children, lest they become discouraged. (Colossians 3:12–14, 18–21)

Here's the secret to living a good news life right at home. It is precisely in the family, because of sheer proximity, that we sin against others the most, that we make the most visible mistakes. If we take ourselves too seriously, our lives can be most unbearable. The Gospel of free forgiveness in Christ frees us to expect mistakes, forgive them, and to find the humor in them after the fact. For me the greatest joy comes when I'm forced to laugh at myself with my family and friends (and sometimes even a dog or two) guffawing and howling just as loudly around the kitchen table.

Study Questions:

Read or sing: "Oh, Blest the House" (*LSB* 862).

1. How does the re-telling of the episode with the BB gun illustrate the joy of life together in the family?
2. Read Colossians 3:12–14; 18–21. How is this passage "a prescription for joy in the family"? What are Christians told to "put on"? How is forgiveness at the center of life together? How does love provide harmony?
3. Read Psalm 127:3–5. How does David in the Psalms describe the joy of children?
4. Read Psalm 128:3 and 6. How are grandchildren a joy and blessing from the Lord?

Something to Think About:

"It is joy in the life of the church-community led by Christ, in the common possession of faith, in familial love in social relations, as well as in the life of faith of others and in the increase of members."

DIETRICH BONHOEFFER, "JOY IN EARLY CHRISTIANITY," *DBW* 9:38

The Joy of Humor

10

Luther's humor is as legendary as it is well documented. It was definitely one way in which he dealt with all the stress he suffered in life. Humor had a profound religious significance for him. Because of the security of the Gospel and the consequent knowledge and conviction that eternity is ours in Christ, Luther believed deeply that we could and should laugh at ourselves, others, and especially the devil in this "mean time." As Gritsch puts it,

> Luther was confident that Christ would triumph over the devil, and so he remained cheerful in his eschatological orientation. . . . Thus he summarized his difficult and busy life in words that exhibited a gallows humor with a scatological twist. "I'm like a ripe stool," he said to his wife Katie shortly before his death, "and the world's like a gigantic anus, and we're about to let go of each other." [Eric Gritsch, *The Wit of Martin Luther* (Fortress Press, 2006), 5]

I love humor. I love to laugh. I love to hear and tell jokes. I love it when others laugh. I love to laugh with others at stupid things I've done. I especially enjoy self-deprecating humor and oxymorons. I find it particularly delightful when both are brought together.

"As a synodical bureaucrat, I am, after all, deeply and profoundly shallow."

The Bible uses specific words for the kind of joy we find in good humor, often translating them as "cheerfulness" or "merry-making" or "celebration." So Luke's Gospel recounts the happy father (an obvious reference to the giddy joy of God over a sinner who repents) saying, *"Let us eat and celebrate. For this my son was lost, and is found. And they began to celebrate"* (Luke 15:23–24). God gives *"wine to gladden the heart of man"* (Psalm 104:15). And it's no accident that in his first miracle Jesus provided an additional one hundred and fifty gallons of wine for a wedding celebration. *"Everyone serves the good wine first, and when people have drunk freely, then the poor wine. But you have kept the good wine until now"* (John 2:10). This miracle both affirms God's good gifts of creation (marriage, celebration

Luther recognized that "since it is from others, humor tells us that life has meaning only in communion with others, and egotistic self-reliance is ridiculous. Really living begins with freedom from the tyranny of the self."

with others, and joy), and indicates that such joy and celebration (good humor) is a foretaste of heaven. To be sure, these texts affirm joy and good humor within a Christian context, but that's because healthy Christianity affirms the good gifts of God's reconciled creation. And humor is such a marvelous gift.

A good joke often presents a paradox. One wouldn't expect the great Reformer to depict his deepest convictions about passing from time to eternity in such, well, "earthy" language. The serious conviction exhibited is in paradoxical tension with the metaphor used to bear the truth. But that's what delights. God has created our minds to find joy in the paradoxical and unexpected.

A paradox is a seemingly sound piece of reasoning based on seemingly true assumptions that leads to a contradiction or another obviously false conclusion. In slightly different words, this could be the definition of a joke. . . . There is something absurd about true stuff that leads ever so logically to false stuff; and absurd is funny. Holding two mutually contradicting ideas in our heads at the same time makes us giddy. [*Plato and a Platypus Walk into a Bar . . . Understanding Philosophy through Jokes*, © 2007, Thomas Cathcart & Daniel Klein. Published by Harry N. Abrams, Inc., New York. All rights reserved.]

But just because something is humorous, doesn't mean it's not profound. Some years ago in the St. Louis area two boys were shooting rifles. The one boy accidentally shot and killed the other, then was so overcome by the tragedy that he quickly took his own life. The pain and suffering of the families is unimaginable. An older man who knew the boys showed up at the funeral and sat in the back. He was a humble farmer, wearing his bib overalls. Sharing the grief of the family, he hugged the parents, only to have the straps on his overalls unsnap. His "bibs" fell to his ankles revealing his outrageous heart-patterned boxer shorts. The sight was so comical the mourners burst out laughing and couldn't stop. Later, the mother of one of the boys expressed her profound thankfulness for the absurd event. "It showed us all that we would be able to laugh again, even in the midst of the pain." (Bryan Salminen pointed out this story to me.) Humor is "the shock-absorber of life," said Peggy Noonan; "It helps us over the rough spots." In fact, humor is a profound, divine gift, the gift of finding joy in contradictions, of which life presents so very many.

And humor is more than just psychologically or spiritually healthy. Marshall Brain notes:

We've long known that the ability to laugh is helpful to those coping with major illness and the stress of life's problems. But researchers are now saying laughter can do a lot more—it can basically bring balance to all the components of the immune system, which helps us fight off diseases. . . .

Laughter reduces levels of certain stress hormones. In doing this, laughter provides a safety valve that shuts off the flow of stress hormones and the fight-or-flight compounds that swing into action in our bodies when we experience stress, anger, or hostility. These stress hormones suppress the immune system, increase the number of blood platelets (which can cause obstructions in arteries), and raise blood pressure. When we're laughing, natural killer cells that destroy tumors and viruses increase, as do Gamma-interferon (a disease-fighting protein), T-cells, which are a major part of the immune response, and B-cells, which make disease-destroying antibodies. . . .

Good humor is for the Christian a healthy indication that we know the Gospel and that this life is serious business, but not so serious we can't laugh at ourselves and others.

What may surprise you even more is the fact that researchers estimate that laughing a hundred times is equal to ten minutes on the rowing machine or fifteen minutes on an exercise bike. Laughing can be a total body workout! Blood pressure is lowered, and there is an increase in vascular blood flow and in oxygenation of the blood, which further assists healing. Laughter also gives your diaphragm and abdominal, respiratory, facial, leg and back muscles a workout. That's why you often feel exhausted after a long bout of laughter—you've just had an aerobic workout!

The psychological benefits of humor are quite amazing, according to doctors and nurses who are members of the American Association for Therapeutic Humor. People often store negative emotions, such as anger, sadness, and fear, rather than expressing them. Laughter provides a way for these emotions to be harmlessly released. Laughter is cathartic. (Marshall Brain, Howitworks.com)

Luther's delight in joking with his wife or interacting with his house guests and friends is so well known because for much of his professional life several of his table guests made notes about his comments, serious and jocular. (See "Luther's Table Talk," in *Luther's Works*, volume 54.) Gritsch notes that Luther's good humor was grounded in Christian freedom from condemnation and the realization that "since the ultimate is constantly in sight, the penultimate is no longer deadly serious" (Gritsch, *The Wit of Martin Luther*, 78). But Gritsch makes another extraordinary point. Because Luther found "sanity" outside himself in Christ—"this need for outside intervention to shore up sanity"—Luther recognized that "since it is from others, humor tells us that life has meaning only in communion with others, and egotistic self-reliance is ridiculous. Really living begins with freedom from the tyranny of the self" (Gritsch, *The Wit of Martin Luther*, 9)

We've been created to laugh. It's healthy. We've been re-created to laugh even more. Good humor is for the Christian a healthy indication that we know the Gospel and that this life is serious business, but not so serious that we can't laugh at ourselves and others. And a good, round belly laugh with our friends or family or rank strangers reminds us that ultimate joy comes to us from without, from Christ; and penultimate joy comes from the wonderful, interesting and sometimes crazy people with whom he surrounds us. And such joy "must be shared in order to be properly enjoyed" [William Morrice, *Joy in the New Testament* (Eerdmans, 1984), 78].

A man is worried that his wife is losing her hearing, so he consults a doctor. The doctor suggests that he try a simple at-home test on her: Stand behind her and ask her a question, first from twenty feet away, next from ten feet, and finally right behind her.

So the man goes home and sees his wife in the kitchen facing the stove. He says from the door, "What's for dinner tonight?"

No answer.

Ten feet behind her, he repeats, "What's for dinner tonight?"

Still no answer.

Finally, right behind her he says, "What's for dinner tonight?"

And his wife turns around and says, "For the third time— chicken!"

Study Questions:

Read or sing: "Joyful, Joyful We Adore Thee" (*LSB* 803).
1. What is the spiritual significance of humor?
2. How does the Bible testify to the place of joy and celebration in life? Check out these texts: Luke 15:23–24, Psalm 104:15, John 2:10.
3. What is paradox? How do our minds find paradox in humor?
4. How did Luther's understanding of Christian freedom allow him to embrace humor and use humor?

Something to Think About:

One should let God be God, Luther insisted, and not wrest heaven from God. Prayer outweighs pondering divine mysteries; and humorous musings about earthly riddles keeps one's spiritual health better than various remedies of spiritual self-help. Humor is part of the power of the future promised to faithful disciples of Christ. Looking back, they can sing the ancient biblical song in the future tense: We will be like those who dream, and our mouth will be filled with laughter (Ps. 126:1–2).

ERIC GRITSCH, *THE WIT OF MARTIN LUTHER* (FORTRESS, 2006), 115

The Joy of Worship

11

Life is too narrow really, our heart too small, for us to be able to apprehend, let alone comprehend this tremendous joy. For one's heart really to be able to embrace it would cause it to burst and die.

MARTIN LUTHER, *THE HOUSE POSTILS*, 1:117–118

What is it that makes Christian joy, and the joy of worship, so profound, so expansive, so freeing, so . . . well, joyful? For me it's the continued surprise and wonder of not being rejected by Christ. It's the delight of being invited into his presence—not to perform or recount my deeds, but to be forgiven and accepted precisely as a sinner, to hear of the deeds of Christ recounted for me and be the recipient of those deeds here and now. My heart and mind are struck ever new, and constructed anew, in ways I cannot predict. I come burdened, I leave in joy. Greatest wonder of wonders, the Lord rejoices precisely over sinners! *"He will rejoice over thee with joy!"* (Zephaniah 3:17)

Jesus illustrates this joy of worship, and the killjoy of Pharisaism.

> He also told this parable to some who trusted in themselves that they were righteous, and treated others with contempt: "Two men went up into the temple to

pray, one a Pharisee and the other a tax collector. The Pharisee, standing by himself, prayed thus: 'God, I thank you that I am not like other men, extortioners, unjust, adulterers, or even like this tax collector. I fast twice a week; I give tithes of all that I get.' But the tax collector, standing far off, would not even lift up his eyes to heaven, but beat his breast, saying, 'God, be merciful to me, a sinner!' I tell you, this man went down to his house justified, rather than the other." (Luke 18:9–14)

The Pharisee found a hollow, prideful joy in himself. He came to the temple to joyfully boast in himself and left condemned for the very acts of worship he thought were his greatest honor. Braggadocious worship always brings contempt for another sinner. *"Those who are well have no need of a physician, but those who are sick. Go and learn what this means, 'I desire mercy, and not sacrifice.' For I came not to call the righteous, but sinners"* (Matthew 9:12–13).

Paul uses a well-known cognate fifty-five times for "joy" or "rejoice" (*kauxaomai*). It means "joyful boasting" [William Morrice, *Joy in the New Testament* (Eerdmans, 1984), 112–113]. It can mean a "joyful boasting" in Christ and his grace, his salvation, his action, his saving, and in whatever glorifies Christ and his mercy (2 Corinthians 11:30). In the negative, the word depicts prideful boasting in "the flesh" (2 Corinthians 12:1, 5; Philippians 3:3). "For Paul then, as for the Old Testament . . . the element of trust is primary. . . . This means that self-confidence is radically excluded from 'joyfully boasting in God.' There is only one legitimate 'joyful boasting in God,' namely 'through our Lord Jesus Christ'" (Romans 5:11) [Gerhard Kittel, *Theological Dictionary of the New Testament* (Eerdmans, 1964) 3:649].

Notice the tax collector (notoriously despised "sinners" in ancient Israel; Matthew 9:11). He comes with face cast down in shame, pleading for mercy. Yet it is he who goes away "justified." Like

Zachaeus (Luke 19:1), he left forgiven, freed, and changed. The secret of living a good news life in a bad news world—the secret to true joy in worship—is too see ourselves in the tax collector, but also to recognize full well that we are more like the Pharisee than we want to admit. How many times I've heard after a sermon, "Pastor, I'm glad you made that point. So-and-so was in church and really needed to hear that." Few of us would say that, but we think

How many times I've heard after a sermon, "Pastor, I'm glad you made that point. So-and-so was in church and really needed to hear that." Most of us would not say that, but we think it. That is a sure fire killjoy.

it. That is a sure-fire killjoy. Real joy has found mercy in *Christ's* sacrifice! It finds joy in Christ's forgiveness, and joy in Christ's mercy for fellow sinners. Prideful boasting against our neighbor is sure proof of prideful boasting against God. Refusing grace to the neighbor is the sure indicator of a joy-killing refusal of grace from our Savior.

Joy is the glorious, snow-capped peak on a mountain founded upon a death—Christ's. On top of Christ's death is ours in Christ (repentance). The road to joy in worship is through death to resurrection, ours and Christ's. *"Looking to Jesus, the founder and perfecter of our faith, who for the joy that was set before him endured the cross"* (Hebrews 12:2). When Christ's death proclaimed (1 Corinthians 1:23) falls out of preaching, joy begins a serious, inward death spiral.

> The rejoicing over salvation becomes egotistically, factiously, fanatically, zealotically distorted when it detaches itself from the remembrance of Jesus' sacrificial death [Peter Brunner, *Worship in the Name of Jesus* (Concordia, 1968), 189].

The Divine Service is the antidote. It opens with the joyous name "Father, Son, and Holy Spirit," which opens all heaven's joy for us. God's name is then spoken in the absolution, which splashes us parched sinners with baptismal joy all over again. "*With joy shall ye draw water out of the wells of salvation*" (Isaiah 12:3). A word of Law (in the confession of sins, and in the readings and sermon) drums us down hard into hell. But the very same word which raised Lazarus bespeaks us living and joyous again ("*Lazarus come out!*"; John 11:43). The Lord's Supper anchors the Gospel in Christ's sacrifice, recalled ("on the night when he was betrayed"), reclaimed ("given for you"), recounted and, above all, actually applied ("Take, eat . . ."). "In thy *presence* is fullness of joy; at thy right hand there are pleasures for evermore" (Psalm 16:11; KJV).

I found in an old, musty, Lutheran tome a wonderful definition of joy in the face of suffering (i.e., "attached to the remembrance of Jesus' sacrificial death"). All of it applies directly to worship. Unlike the confined, self-aggrandizing focus of the Pharisee, which narrows the heart toward the neighbor, in true joy "the heart is broadened"—broadened to Christ, to grace, to the Church, to others inside and outside the Church. Joy is broad! "*You are not restricted by us, but you are restricted in your own affections. . . . widen your hearts also*" (2 Corinthians 6:12–13).

The musty Lutheran writes:

> "Rejoice that you suffer with Christ" (1 Peter 4:13). "Rejoice" [*chairete*] says the apostle, "let this be for you a true, hearty joy." Joy is an affect and emotion, where the heart is broadened. Joy accepts the present good and is heartily, completely, and delightfully satisfied over it. Future good is expected in heartfelt joy. As now all joy, to which the corrupt nature drives us, is corrupt and impure; so on the contrary a pure and holy joy is a working of the grace of God, when the mere joy of the world

becomes ever more bitter. On the contrary, the divine things begin to delight and to satisfy us. Here, Peter calls such a spiritual joy of the heart, amidst cross and trials, a [true] joy, which happens in the Lord Jesus. Reason understands nothing of it, but faith conceives of such joy because it does not look to the visible and temporal, but rather to the invisible and eternal (2 Corinthians 4:18). Indeed, this appears to be a paradox [*paradoxon*] and rare matter, to have joy in the midst of suffering. [Johann Gottfried Palm, *Erklärung der ersten und andern Epistel Petri* (Dresden, 1731), 919 f.; translation by M.H.]

It's all profound, but very simple. The Prodigal was all about freedom sans love. He ended up a slave to himself. The Judaizers were all about following the Law sans freedom, and they lost the Gospel too! Freedom and love belong together in Christian worship and life.

It is a great irony that worship—the foretaste of future good expected in heartfelt joy—should be cause for division in the Church, that hearts should be narrowed rather than broadened in freedom and love. The problem is as old as the narrowed, self-centered heart revealed in the parable of the Pharisee and the tax collector—as old as the challenge of worship run-amok in Corinth (1 Corinthians 11–14) or legalism in Galatia. *"Now the works of the flesh are . . . enmity, strife, jealousy, fits of anger, rivalries, dissensions, divisions. . . . But the fruit of the Spirit is love, joy, peace, patience, kindness, goodness, faithfulness, gentleness, self-control"* (Galatians 5:19 ff.).

There are two simple, joyous truths about worship from Scripture. The first truth is that in Christ there is freedom in worship! The second truth is that true Christian freedom expresses itself in love. Notice how the apostles combine these two basic bedrock truths of the New Testament! *"For you were called to freedom, brothers. Only do not use your freedom as an opportunity for the flesh, but through love serve one another"* (Galatians 5:13; cf. 1 Peter 2:16). It's all profound, but very simple. The Prodigal was all about freedom sans love. He ended up a slave to himself. The Judaizers were all about following the Law sans freedom, and they lost the Gospel too! Freedom and love belong together in Christian worship and life.

So Lutherans always have and always will recognize the very broad freedom in worship. "It is not necessary for the true unity of the Christian Church that ceremonies, instituted by human beings, should be observed uniformly in all places" (Augsburg Confession VII). Luther even wrote, "Everything in the Mass (i.e. "the service") up to the Creed is ours, free and not prescribed by God" (*Luther's Works*, 53:25). But freedom bereft of love ends in joyless self-centeredness.

Regarding what in worship is neither commanded nor forbidden by the Word of God, *"All things are lawful,' but not all things are helpful. 'All things are lawful,' but not all things build up"* (1 Corinthians 10:23). Martin Luther applied his famous dictum in his important Reformation tract, "The Freedom of the Christian Man," to the issue of worship, and both the Augsburg Confession (AC VII) and the Formula of Concord (FC SD X 9) followed:

> A Christian is a perfectly free lord of all, subject to none.
> A Christian is a perfectly dutiful servant of all, subject to all (*Luther's Works*, 33:344).

Freedom exercised in love is the hallmark of Lutheran worship. While I prefer the predominant use of a Lutheran hymnal, I recognize that the boundaries of acceptable practice are broader than my own preferences. On the other hand, the individual and the individual congregation—in matters of worship—must always act in ways which serve the neighbor in love. Nothing that impedes or distorts the Gospel can endure in worship.

> Love is patient and kind; love does not envy or boast; it is not arrogant or rude. It does not insist on its own way; it is not irritable or resentful; it does not rejoice (*chairei*) at wrongdoing, but rejoices (*synchairei*) with the truth. Love bears all things, believes all things, hopes all things, endures all things (1 Corinthians 13:4–7).

There's the joyous secret.

Study Questions:

Read or sing: "O Bride of Christ, Rejoice" (*LSB* 335).

1. Luther speaks of how the human heart is far too small to apprehend the tremendous joy of Christ. In another sermon he comments to the effect that if our hearts would truly take in the full significance of Christmas, they would break into a hundred thousand pieces. What makes the joy of Christ so explosive?
2. We come to the Divine Service with the burdens and anxieties of our sin, and we leave in the joy of sin forgiven. How is Zephaniah 3:17 descriptive of our joy in worship?
3. The joy of worship is the opposite of the false joy of the Pharisees. How is this illustrated in Luke 18:9–14?
4. How does Matthew 9:12–13 give focus to the Church's mission?
5. What does Paul mean by "joyful boasting"? See 2 Corinthians 11:30; 12:1, 5; Philippians 3:3.
6. Read Luke 19:1–10. What does Zacchaeus teach us about joy?
7. Read 1 Corinthians 1:23. What happens to joy when the death of Christ falls out of preaching?

8. Peter Brunner says "The rejoicing over salvation becomes egotistically, fanatically, zealotically distorted when it detaches itself from the remembrance of Jesus' sacrificial death." How can this happen in the life of the Church? What is the remedy?
9. What do Isaiah 12:3 and Psalm 16:11 teach us about joy in worship?
10. How does the citation from Johann Gottfried Palm stretch our understanding of joy in the face of suffering?
11. What "two simple joyous truths about worship" are expressed in the New Testament? How might these truths shape decisions about liturgy in the Lutheran congregation?
12. What happens to joy when freedom ignores love? See Galatians 5:13 and 1 Peter 2:16.

Something to Think About:

"Here the sacrament is the communion among brethren whose joy is one another. Joy in the sacraments—that is the joy of the heart full of longing and desire for its God whom it has found; that is the anticipation of the strangers, the homeless, as they look forward to their eternal home and pray that it may come."

DIETRICH BONHOEFFER, "ASCENSION DAY SERMON 1933," *DBW* 12:470

The Joy of Life

12

The joy over the gift of life shines brightest against the darkness of deadly evil.

In October 1939, Adolf Hitler signed a brief directive empowering his personal physician and another henchman the power of "extending to specified doctors that those who, according to human judgment, are incurably ill may be granted, after a critical examination of the state of their health, a 'mercy death.'" Families began to complain about obituaries of their institutionalized loved ones, appearing suddenly in the newspapers. Because of protests from the staffs of churchly institutions, the SS began transporting the mentally ill or disabled to state institutions first before euthanization (murder). A few courageous churchmen protested, including Lutheran Friedrich von Bodelschwingh (1877–1946; a close associate of Herman Sasse) of the Bethel Institute. He repeatedly scrambled to find homes for children (often Jewish children) slated for "elimination." Roman Catholic bishop, Clemens August Graf von Galen (1876–1946), preached publicly denouncing the murders, which were now being extended to the aged infirm.

> Do you or I have the right to live only as long as we are productive? . . . Then someone has only to order a secret decree that the measures tried out on the mentally ill be extended to the other "nonproductive" people, that it can

be used on those incurably ill with lung disease, on those weakened by aging, on those disabled at work, on severely wounded soldiers. Then not a one of us is sure anymore of his life . . . Woe to humanity, woe to our German people, when the sacred commandment "Thou shalt not kill" is not only violated, but when this violation is tolerated and carried out without punishment [Victoria Barnett, *For the Soul of the People: Protestant Protest Against Hitler* (Oxford, 1992), 117 ff.].

The British dropped leaflets of Galen's sermon over the towns and villages. Hitler's murderous secret was secret no more. Under public pressure, twenty-one days after the bishop's sermon, the madman ordered the carnage to cease. The records show that 70,273 patients had been murdered, though the actual count was probably much higher.

Lutheran pastor, Ernst Wilm (1901–89), a former vicar of von Bodelschwingh at Bethel, had also dared to protest publicly. He rejoiced that the killing had apparently ended and thanked God for it in his New Year's Eve sermon of 1942. But the rumors commenced again later that month. So did Wilm. He recounted:

I was arrested on January 23, 1942 and interrogated, basically, only because of this story about the killings of patients. They asked me about little things: why I didn't say *"Heil Hitler"* when I came to the confirmation class. It was ludicrous. And they said, "You're stabbing the army in the back with such stories." I replied, "You're stabbing the army in the back when you murder children and sick people behind the backs of the men and fathers who are out there." I came to the police prison in Bielefeld and sat there until May. Then came the command, signed by

Heydrich, and with that, I came to Dachau and served my time there. (Barnett, *For the Soul of the People*, 117 ff.)

Wilm was sentenced to the infamous concentration camp in May 1942. The number 30,156 was tattooed on his forearm. He was released only to be conscripted, and was soon captured by the Russians. It's a miracle he survived. *"Rescue the weak and the needy; deliver them from the hand of the wicked"* (Psalm 82:4).

. . . each and every human life is temporally and eternally precious, no matter how young, old, or imperfect. The secret to a joyous life worth living is acting on behalf of those who cannot act for themselves.

The Nazis called "the weak and the needy," "lives unworthy of living." The secret of living a good news life in a bad news world, is knowing that every human being is created in God's own image and is therefore valuable. The secret to a joyous and meaningful life is the realization that because Jesus himself took on human flesh, from conception, and because Jesus valued every human life (especially those "worthless" in the eyes of the world), each and every human life is temporally and eternally precious, no matter how young, old, or imperfect. The secret to a joyous life worth living is acting on behalf of those who cannot act for themselves.

Joy over life verily leaps off the pages of holy writ. It bubbles from the mouth of Jesus. It animates his every action. There is—in addition to specific, pervasive, and persuasive texts (Genesis 1:26, 27; 9:6; Exodus 21:22–25)—an ethic of the inherent value of every human life conceived, no matter its form or malformity. Simply put, for Jesus there is no "life unworthy of life." In fact, the Christ turns the human value system completely on its head (1 Corinthians 1:25, 27), to the great delight and joy of the "least."

> And when Elizabeth heard the greeting of Mary, the baby leaped [*eskiptasen;* "skipped!"] in her womb. And Elizabeth was filled with the Holy Spirit, and she exclaimed with a loud cry, "Blessed are you among women, and blessed is the fruit of your womb! And why is this granted to me that the mother of my Lord should come to me? For behold, when the sound of your greeting came to my ears, the baby in my womb leaped for joy [*eskiptasen en agalliasei*] (Luke 1:41-44).

What a remarkable transaction! John the Baptizer "skips for joy" *in utero* over the greeting of "the mother of my Lord." Two un-borns (the Lord himself and his great forerunner) are each acknowledged as such in the womb! The word (used by Luke more than any other New Testament writer) expresses what is an "outburst of joy" (*agallian*). Luke is indeed the "evangelist of joy," and more. He's the "evangelist of the joy over life!" Allow me to pass briefly through only a portion of Luke's Gospel, looking through the lens of this "preferential option" for the least—Jesus' joy over life.

A peasant, Elizabeth, rejoiced over the unborn Lord (Luke 1:42). The unlikely mother of the Lord, Mary, sang her "Magnificat": *"My spirit rejoices in God my Savior. . . . he has exalted those of humble estate"* (Luke 1:46ff.). Elizabeth's friends and family rejoiced with her over her newborn (Luke 1:58). Zechariah's tongue was loosed in praise after the mute wrote, *"His name is John. . . . He spoke, blessing God . . . for [God] has visited and redeemed his people"* (Luke 1:63, 64, 68). Praise and blessing are the sounds that joy makes!

At the birth of Christ, the angel announced to the shepherds: *"Fear not, for behold, I bring you good news of a great joy that will be for all the people"* (Luke 2:10). The whole heavenly host rejoiced over the One who came to bring peace between God and man (Luke 2:14). Feeble old Simeon beheld this very life—in his own arms, in the flesh, and rejoiced! *"Mine eyes have seen your salvation.*

. . . Let your servant depart in peace" (Luke 2:29). Peace is joy at rest.

Jesus (a quiet man, a carpenter from Nazareth) suddenly came preaching a message of joy, particularly for the outcast, the weak, the lame, for the "lives unworthy of life": *"He has sent me to proclaim liberty to the captives and recovering of sight to the blind, to set at liberty those who are oppressed, to proclaim the year of the Lord's favor"* (Luke 4:18–19). He immediately set upon his path of caring for the sick and needy (Simon's mother-in-law, Luke 4:38f.; the sick and diseased, Luke 4:40f.; the paralytic, Luke 5:25f.; and the leper, Luke 5:12f.).

Simply put, for Jesus there is no "life unworthy of life." In fact, the Christ turns the human value system completely on its head (1 Corinthians 1:25, 27), to the great delight and joy of the "least."

Then Jesus began inviting the dregs of society to be his friends (like Levi, the tax collector; Luke 5:27f.), and he still invites us to join the dregs! *"Those who are well have no need of a physician, but those who are sick"* (Luke 5:31). Luke tells us that he feasted and rejoiced with them all, and thereby honored life as a gift (Luke 5:34–36). Jesus, the very ambassador of life, taught that any law which compromised and threatened life had to fall (Luke 6:1ff.). *"I ask you, is it lawful on the Sabbath to do good or to do harm, to save life or to destroy it?"* (Luke 6:9). He made the ambassadors of death furious over his joy for life and for the least (Luke 6:11). The multitudes came to him—diseased and with unclean spirits—and were healed. Life so pulsated in and pervaded his life that when they merely touched him, he "healed them all" (Luke 6:19). Has there ever been such respect for life?

He expressed his attitude of joy over the oppressed, the least, the worst, the hungry, the sad, the sinner, in beatitude after beatitude.

Only the merciless escaped his mercy. *"Blessed are you who weep now, for you shall laugh"* (Luke 6:21). He bid his disciples rejoice at being reviled for his name's sake. And they did (1 Peter 4:13; Acts 5:41; Acts 9:16). *"Rejoice in that day, and leap for joy, for behold, your reward is great in heaven; for so their fathers did to the prophets"* (Luke 6:23). Even enemies have lives worth living! *"Be merciful to all, even enemies!"* (Luke 6:31). Christ is God incarnate, Joy in the flesh, Life, sent to redeem life. His joy for life, over life, tells us who our God is. *"Be merciful, even as your Father is merciful"* (Luke 6:36). The centurion's daughter (Luke 7:8ff), the widow's son (Luke 7:12ff.), the blind, the lame, the lepers, the deaf, the poor—all were healed and heard the Gospel again and again (Luke 7:21ff.). The least are the greatest in the kingdom (Luke 7:46f.). Jesus ate and drank and enjoyed time with his band of misfits, "tax collectors and sinners" and even prostitutes (Luke 7:34; 7:49; 8:1ff.). The "good soil" is, according to Jesus, the refuse of the world, the despised of the world. The good news knows no genetic preference (Luke 8:9ff., 19). The Gerasene—after so much pain and suffering, joyless and "dead" while he lived in the cemetery, dragging his chains—was put at rest, *"sitting at the feet of Jesus, clothed and in his right mind"* (Luke 8:35). The poor woman whose livelihood had been exhausted by hemorrhage, was healed—finally healed in both body and soul after twelve joyless years (Luke 8:41ff.). Jairus' daughter was raised—life from death (Luke 8:54–55)!

Jesus preached that he would be killed but *"on the third day be raised"* (Luke 9:22). Because he would pass from death to life, he invited his followers on the path to joy, to deny themselves and follow him. *"Whoever loses his life for my sake will save it"* (Luke 9:23). How did Jesus "lose" his life? By spending it for others, by sharing the burdens, suffering, and joys and sorrows of others. Jesus healed the boy with epilepsy (Luke 9:39). In Jesus' ethic of life, the least are the greatest, the despised are precious. *"Whoever receives this child in my name receives me, and whoever receives me receives him who sent me. For he who is least among you all is the one who is great"* (Luke 9:48). Jesus was "exuberant with joy," along with the returning seventy-two (Luke 10:17f.) over the good news preached and the needy healed. He "rejoiced exuberantly in the Holy Spirit"—joyously confessed it a marvel that such things had been revealed to "little children" but not the wise (Luke 10:21). In the parable of the Good Samaritan, Jesus taught that life is precious no matter whose it is (Luke 10:35f).

There is much, much more in Luke's Gospel alone, including all the rejoicing over the prodigal, the lost coin, the great banquet . . . and finally, the greatest affirmation of human life in time for eternity, the resurrection of Jesus. After the Lord's ascension *"they worshiped him and returned to Jerusalem with great joy, and were continually in the temple blessing God"* (Luke 24:52–53). Acts continues the exuberant theme of joy over life (Acts 2:26, 46; 5:41; 8:8, 39; 11:23; 12:14; 13:52). *"In all things I [Paul] have shown you that by working hard in this way we must help the weak and remember the words of the Lord Jesus, how he himself said, 'It is more blessed to give than to receive'"* (Acts 20:35). Each and every one of these references is a testament etched in stone bearing witness: there is no "life unworthy of living"!

There were 70,273 patients murdered under Hitler. There have been some 50 million abortions since Roe vs. Wade was decided in the U.S. Supreme Court in 1973. A large percentage of those aborted have been children suspected of deformity or disability. *"They will have no mercy on the fruit of the womb"* (Isaiah 13:18). I must confess, I find joy at this very point to be most elusive. I am part of a culture which condones the death of the innocent. In fact (unlike Hitler with the mentally ill and infirm), it quite openly and dramatically asserts there is "life unworthy of living."

"Deliver me from blood guiltiness, O God, O God of my salvation, and my tongue will sing aloud of your righteousness" (Psalm 51:14). James confessed, *"Religion that is pure and undefiled before God, the*

Father, is this: to visit orphans and widows in their affliction, and to keep oneself unstained from the world" (James 1:27). Isaiah points us on our path: *"Learn to do good; seek justice, correct oppression; bring justice to the fatherless, plead the widow's cause"* (Isaiah 1:17). There's the secret to rejoicing over the gift of life.

Study Questions:

Read or sing: "My Soul Now Magnifies the Lord" (*LSB* 934).

1. How is the Nazi logic of disposing of "lives unworthy of life" disrupting the joy of life in our own day?
2. What do the Scriptures teach us about the value of all human life, including the lives of the weak and helpless? See Genesis 1:26–27; 9:6; Exodus 21:22–25.
3. Read Luke 1:44. How does the unborn John the Baptist react to Mary's greeting?
4. Mary responds to the angelic announcement that she will be the mother of the Savior with a canticle we have come to know as the Magnificat. Read Luke 1:46–55. What does her hymn tell us about joy?
5. How does Luke 2:29–32 demonstrate the truth of the definition that "peace is joy at rest"?
6. The messianic manifesto for Jesus' ministry is recorded in Luke 4:18–19. How does this text describe the joy of the salvation brought by Jesus? How does Luke's Gospel document Jesus' joy-restoring work?
7. Read Luke 24:52–53. Jesus' ascension to the right hand of the Father does not mean that he is absent from us. Where the Lord is, there is joy. How do the disciples respond to the ascension?

8. Where the joy of the Lord is, there will be merciful service of the neighbor in the way of James 1:27. How are we to show forth this joy in a world which seems set on destroying the unborn (Isaiah 13:18), the disabled, and the aged?

Something to Think About:

"Every Christian community must know that not only do the weak need the strong, but also the strong cannot exist without the weak. The elimination of the weak is the death of the community. The Christian community should not be governed by self-justification, which violates others, but by justification by grace, which serves others. Once individuals have experienced the mercy of God in their lives, from then on they desire only to serve. The proud throne of the judge no longer lures them; instead they want to be down among the wretched and lowly, because God found them down there themselves. 'Do not be haughty, but associate with the lowly'" (Romans 12:16).

DIETRICH BONHOEFFER, *LIFE TOGETHER* (FORTRESS, 2005), 96

The Joy of All Creation

13

The heavens declare the glory of God and the sky above proclaims his handiwork. . . . [The sun] comes out like a bridegroom leaving his chamber, and, like a strong man, runs its course with joy.

PSALM 19:1, 5

Have you seen Ben Stein's movie, Expelled? It was the top documentary of 2008. The show highlights a growing debate within the scientific academy over the issue of "Intelligent Design." Darwin's evolutionary theories were formed before we knew anything of the human genome, DNA, microbiology, Einstein's theory of relativity, or before we could evaluate (via computer) the probabilities of random microbiological events required to produce life from its tiniest building blocks to its most complex forms. Dr. David Berlinski (neither a Christian or a creationist, and a star of the Stein movie), "refers to Francis Crick, who with Watson discovered the structure of DNA, saying that the 'cumulative improbabilities are so staggering' [of life coming to exist by chance] that Crick concluded it more likely that life was sent here from outer space, a view called 'directed panspermia.'" (alivingdog.com/Berlinski) "Panspermia"? Sent from outer space? Ah . . . that would be from aliens, right?

For decades, scientist have been listening to deep space for any evidence of intelligence, e.g., ordered radio waves. What have they found? Nothing. What was self-evident to the greatest minds in history (Christian and non-), what was "self-evident truth" to the founders of the United States (Christian and non-) was that the ordered complexity of the observable world, including an inherent moral order, bore witness to a Creator.

If life is a result of chance occurrence, if the universe is a result of random events, then all of human social, moral, and religious life is a construct. There simply is nothing external to humankind itself which is in any way truth (aside from the "truth" of the principles of natural selection).

If life is a result of chance occurrence, if the universe is a result of random events, then all of human social, moral, and religious life is a construct. There simply is nothing external to humankind itself which is in any way truth (aside from the "truth" of the principles of natural selection). Marriage, for instance (as many now hold), would be a construct, which has evolved in a certain way (man-woman) based upon competing forces and is undergoing a evolutionary metamorphosis in our time. (See Romans 1:18–32.) Death, then, is quite simply, the end. That's it. The end of each human story and of joy as intended by God.

When man makes himself his own god, a very poor god he makes. "Which of the religions of the world gives to its followers the greatest happiness? While it lasts, the religion of worshiping oneself is best" [C.S. Lewis, *God in the Dock* (Eerdmans, 1994), 58]. But the *happiness* rarely lasts, and never through death. What irony that

- the Lord who has created the universe to reflect his very own infinity and infinite knowledge;
- the very Lord who created the human mind with the curiosity

and capacity to investigate itself and its world;

• the very Lord who rejoices in knowledge, truth, wisdom and understanding, and who loves it when one layer of mystery about the universe falls, only to unveil a thousand more, and invites us to chase the next wonder;

• humankind stares at this same Lord in the face in his creation, as it were, and can't see him at all.

If there is anything the Lord laughs at, that's got to be it. *"He who sits in the heavens laughs; the Lord holds them in derision"* (Psalm 2:4). There may be joy, but it's a joy veiled and curtailed, like receiving a gift but not knowing its giver.

Johann Kepler (1571–1630) consistently makes the list of the greatest scientific minds in history. He's the founder of modern astronomy. Carl Sagan called him the "first astrophysicist." The quest for knowledge of the universe was for him an expedition of sheer, divinely-given joy.

> What is the good of the knowledge of nature, of all astronomy, to a hungry stomach? . . . Painters are allowed to go on with their work because they give joy to eyes, musicians because they bring joy to the ears . . . What insensibility, what stupidity, to deny the spirit an honest pleasure, but permit it to the eyes and ears!
>
> He who fights against this joy fights against nature, . . . Should the kind Creator who brought forth nature out of nothing . . . deprive the spirit of man, the master of creation and the Lord's own image, of every heavenly delight? Do we ask what profit the little bird hopes for in singing? We know that singing in itself is a joy to him because he was created for singing.
>
> We must note therefore why the human spirit takes such trouble to find out the secrets of the skies. . . . Man's soul is kept alive, enriched and grows by that food called

knowledge [Kepler quoted in Frankenberry, Nancy; *The Faith of Scientists*. © 2008 by Princeton University Press. Reprinted by permission of Princeton University Press.]

The Copernican revolution became established science because of Kepler. It was Kepler, studying the orbit of planets, who figured out that there was a force unaccounted for in the rotation of those planets. Isaac Newton—building upon Kepler—described the universal law of gravity. "If I have seen further, it is by standing on the shoulders of Giants." After years of struggle, Kepler figured out the basic laws of planetary motion, discovered and documented the elliptical orbit of planets, and that planets travel faster the closer they come to the focus of their ellipse.

Kepler succeeded Danish Lutheran Tycho Brahe (d. 1601) as court astronomer of Emperor Rudolf II. Despite erroneous accounts to the contrary, Kepler was a devout Lutheran. He wrote to his orthodox professor of theology, Haffenreffer, "I agree with the Augsburg Confession and the Formula of Concord. . . . I am ready to subscribe to the Formula of Concord as a layman." He did not doubt Luther's doctrine of the Sacrament, but had reservations about technical language used in the argumentation regarding the various ways Christ is present in the world. [See Werner Elert, *The Structure of Lutheranism* (Concordia, 1962), 426ff.] The great astronomer's dying words were: "Only the merits of our Savior, Jesus Christ. It is in Him, as I steadfastly testify, that there rest all my retreat, all my consolation, all my hope."

Few people in all of history have so profoundly understood (and all this before the invention of the telescope!) the truth of Psalm 19:1, *"The heavens declare the glory of God; the skies proclaim the work of His hands."* And it produced profound joy! Note the place of joy in a prayer written by the Lutheran genius.

O Thou who through the light of nature does increase in us the longing for the light of Thy Grace, that through it we may come to the light of Thy majesty, I give Thee thanks, Creator and God, that Thou has given me this joy in Thy creation, and I rejoice in the works of Thy hands. See I have now completed the work to which I was called. In it I have used all the talents Thou has lent to my spirit. I have revealed the majesty of Thy works to those men who will read my works, insofar as my narrow understanding can comprehend their infinite richness [Arthur Beer, *Kepler: Four Hundred Years* (Pergamum Press, 1975), 359].

As Kepler's prayer confesses, if there is any discipline packed with joy, it's science! What is more joyous than endless surprise and discovery?! Scientific joy is a First Article joy. "I believe that God has made me and all creatures; that He has given me my body and soul, eyes, ears, and all my members, my reason and all my senses,

For the first time in my life, I beheld a whole galaxy. Horizon to horizon, a one-hundred-eighty-degree swath of a billion stars of the Milky Way, painted like glitter on a swath of black velvet, the blackness of deep space.

and still takes care of them" (Small Catechism, First Article). What a difference it makes when "my reason and all my senses" are not closed to the world about us—but open wide to surprise! Oh, we need young Lutheran men and women to be scientists! And what double joy when we actually know the very name of the God—Father, Son, and Holy Spirit. who created all things (Genesis 1; Colossians 2)!

As classical Christians, we believe that the account of creation in Genesis records history. There is no middle ground here. You don't get very far with a real Adam in a mythical garden, or with a real fall into sin without a first human being. You can't stretch the accounts to cover billions or millions of years and so mesh the biblical account with Darwinism. The order of things created in Genesis does not even follow the order proposed by evolution. The problem of evil is unavoidable, and Darwin presumes death (a fallen state) as a presupposition to the development of human life (survival of the fittest). Genesis is either complete myth, or it is history recorded in the simple language of its time.

But this devotion is not an apology for Intelligent Design, nor for Creationism (which is quite something else); it is a little treatise on finding joy in creation. Much less do we desire to bash scientists or science itself. Not at all! In fact, we sing their praises. We argue that science—like politics, or agriculture, or sociology—is a discipline of the "kingdom of the left," ruled by reason. Kepler, who believed the creation accounts were history, understood these categories. "I have just one thing to say: while in theology it is authority [i.e. of the Bible] that carries the most weight, in philosophy it is reason" (Frankenberry, *The Faith of Scientists*, 53). Agreed!

We Christians have a unique responsibility. It is to rejoice over creation! If we don't, who will? Or who can do so in the way we can? Atheists and agnostics can find joy in discovery and beauty in complexity (and often more so than we do, to our shame!). But they cannot praise the Maker. Theists (whether agnostic or of a non-Christian religion) can appreciate the work of the Creator, but they cannot finally praise the Christ, who with the Father and the Spirit is Creator and Redeemer (Colossians 1:15ff.), in whom all things hold together and find their purpose (Acts 17:22ff.). In our time, says Elert,

> God's creation has been "scientifically" isolated from its Lord. It has become a laboratory, a testing ground for

applied physics, a confiscated apartment for men without a home, reproducible in color photography, measured by light years . . . We can still amuse ourselves but we no longer know how to be happy . . . In one approach creation no longer has a soul, in another approach the soul has sold out to nature. In one way or another man, in spite of his claim of superiority, has become expendable, is at the edge of the world without a future, an atom ready to explode everything or be blown to pieces himself . . . If the Christian can no longer see God's hand in creation, who shall see it? . . . If a Christian can no longer feel joy in God's creation because he, too, has lost hope, the visible beauty, along with the joy, will disappear forever [Werner Elert, *The Christian Ethos* (Muhlenberg, 1957), 320].

The Bible invites us to join its ever-rising crescendo of joy over the created world. In fact, not only does God rejoice in his own creation, not only does humankind rejoice in this blessed creation, but also, according to the Bible, the very creation itself rejoices in the Lord, its Maker and Redeemer. *"The LORD reigneth; let the earth rejoice!"* (Psalm 97:1 KJV) The "Hallel Psalms" (146–150) bear witness to the exuberance of all the earth in joy over Yahweh, "who made heaven and earth" (Psalm 146:6).

Some years ago I found myself flat on my back in a dry, rock-strewn riverbed, hours from anywhere in central Australia. It was a crystal clear, pitch black, moonless night. I beheld the heavens in a spectacular, 3D, high definition, life-sized, living, moving mural. It took my breath away. For the first time in my life, I beheld a whole galaxy. Horizon to horizon, a one-hundred-eighty-degree swath of a billion stars of the Milky Way, painted like glitter on a swath of black velvet, the blackness of deep space.

I was filled with doubt teetering on the edge of belief. *"Where is your God?"* (Psalm 42:10). In the face of infinity, how can I possibly believe that there is a God who is concerned about our tiny planet? How can I believe that there is a God who knows who I am and should even care about me or about any human being? Is there a God at all? Who and what am I? What is my life compared to the universe? I am a micro-speck, a piece of subatomic dust, circling a black hole—a minute piece of finitude, about to be devoured by infinity. *"When I look at your heavens, the work of your fingers, the moon and the stars, which you have set in place, what is man that you are mindful of him, and the son of man that you care for him?"* (Psalm 8:3–4)

But then I began to consider that all I beheld was marvelously ordered. *"Give thanks to him who made the great lights, for his steadfast love endures forever; the sun to rule over the day, for his steadfast love endures forever; the moon and stars to rule over the night, for his steadfast love endures forever"* (Psalm 136:8–9). I was staring God in the face, as it were. No, not God in the flesh, the revealed Son of God, but the same God in nature, nevertheless. *"Is not God high in the heavens?"* (Job 22:12) Yes, to be sure. But this is God who revealed himself to Abram (who had the very same thoughts with which I struggle) and promised him, *"I will multiply your offspring as the stars of heaven . . . And in your offspring all the nations of the earth shall be blessed"* (Genesis 26:4). God used the very thing that terrified Abraham to console him.

There were the familiar southern constellations. . . . Ptolemy was able to study them, was he not? Copernicus studied their northern counterparts. Kepler reveled in them as an act of knowledge, of sacred vocation, of faith and joy all in one. *"Let the heavens be glad, and let the earth rejoice"* (Psalm 96:11). And then I beheld, in my infinite insignificance, the Southern Cross, and my doubt was dashed upon the Bright and Morning Star (Revelation 22:16). *"He determines the number of the stars; he gives to all of them their names"* (Psalm 147:4). And the joy of knowing this God of the heavens in Christ chased back all doubt. *"And behold, the star that they had seen when it rose went before them until it came to rest over the place where the child was. When they saw the star, they rejoiced exceedingly with great joy"* (Matthew 2:9–10).

I look forward to God's handiwork in the heavens becoming harbingers of the consummation of time into eternity, the very resurrection itself! *"And there will be signs in sun, moon and stars"* (Luke 21:25). *"Look up! . . . For your redemption draweth nigh!"* (Luke 21:28 KJV) How can we look away? *"There is one glory of the sun, and another glory of the moon, and another glory of the stars; for star differs from star in glory. . . . So is it with the resurrection of the dead"* (1 Corinthians 15:41ff.). *"Where were you . . . when the morning stars sang together, and all the sons of God shouted for joy?"* (Job 38:4, 7) I'm here now, and I shout: *"Let the heavens be glad, and let the earth rejoice, and let them say among the nations, 'The Lord reigns!' "* (1 Chronicles 16:31)

Oh, had I known Kepler's prayer, I would have prayed it, over and again in joy:

> O Thou, who by the light of nature increases in us the desire for the light of Thy mercy in order to be led by this to Thy glory, to Thee I offer thanks, Creator, God, because Thou hast given me pleasure in what Thou hast created and I rejoice in Thy handiwork [Max Casper, *Kepler* (Dover, 1993), 375].

The secret to living a good news life in a bad news world is marveling with joy at the vast ordered complexity of all creation and recognizing by faith the God (Father, Son, and Holy Spirit) who created it all for our blessed surprise, enjoyment, and faith.

PSALM 96

Oh sing to the Lord a new song; sing to the Lord, all the earth!

Sing to the Lord, bless his name; tell of his salvation from day to day.

Declare his glory among the nations, his marvelous works among all the peoples!

For great is the Lord, and greatly to be praised; he is to be feared above all gods.

For all the gods of the peoples are worthless idols, but the Lord made the heavens.

Splendor and majesty are before him; strength and beauty are in his sanctuary.

Ascribe to the Lord, O families of the peoples, ascribe to the Lord glory and strength!

Ascribe to the Lord the glory due his name; bring an offering, and come into his courts!

Worship the Lord in the splendor of holiness; tremble before him, all the earth!

Say among the nations, "The Lord reigns! Yes, the world is established; it shall never be moved; he will judge the peoples with equity."

Let the heavens be glad, and let the earth rejoice; let the sea roar, and all that fills it;

let the field exult, and everything in it! Then shall all the trees of the forest sing for joy

before the Lord, for he comes, for he comes to judge the earth. He will judge the world in righteousness, and the peoples in his faithfulness.

Study Questions:

Read or sing: "Evening and Morning" (*LSB* 726).

1. Read Psalm 19:1. How do the heavens declare the joy of God?

2. What does Romans 1:18–32 teach us about life in creation after the fall?

3. Reflect on the observation made by C. S. Lewis that "While it lasts, the religion of worshiping oneself" is the best in giving the greatest happiness. Why is it that this happiness finally will not last?

4. How does the Lord react to the vain attempts of humanity to achieve independence from him? See Psalm 2:4.

5. Who was Johann Kepler? How did his faith free him for joy in scientific pursuit and discovery?

6. How does Kepler's prayer reflect the truth of Psalm 19:1?

7. Read Colossians 1:15–20 and Acts 17:22–31. In light of these texts, how is it that Christians have the unique responsibility to rejoice over creation?

8. According to Werner Elert, "God's creation has been 'scientifically' isolated from its Lord" in modernity. How does this rob humanity of joy in creation?

9. Review Psalms 146–150, the so-called "Hallel Psalms." How do these psalms testify to God's joy in creation?

10. Read Psalm 8. The Lutheran theologian, Oswald Bayer, suggest that this psalm establishes man as "both king and child" in the universe. In other words, Psalm 8 gives humanity dignity in creation. How is this dignity a cause for joy as we recognize who we are in God's sight?

11. Read Genesis 26:4. How does God use the very thing that terrified Abraham to console him?

12. We have more than the stars that dot the night skies. Our joy is secure in the Lord who made them. See Psalm 147:4, Matthew 2:9–10.

13. The handiwork of God in the heavens points to the consummation of all things in the return of Christ. How does Luke 21:28 tell us to anticipate the Lord's coming?
14. Read the following Old Testament texts: Job 38:4–7; 1 Chronicles 16:31; and Psalm 96. What does each of these texts teach us about joy in relation to creation?

Something to Think About:

"Delight in Creation is a prerogative of faith."

WERNER ELERT, *THE CHRISTIAN FAITH*
(LUTHERAN THEOLOGICAL SEMINARY, 1974), 166

The Joy of a Faithful Pastor

14

Obey your leaders and submit to them, for they are keeping watch over your souls, as those who will have to give an account. Let them do this with joy and not with groaning, for that would be of no advantage to you. HEBREWS 13:17

A twenty-seven year old missionary bid his friend, Baltimore Lutheran Pastor Haesbaert, goodbye at the train station in Havre de Grace, Maryland. "For the first time, I felt like a stranger in this country." Once again, he found himself struggling against loneliness and melancholy. He had fought these morose feelings since childhood, along with ill health which aggravated them. He would struggle with depression until the day he died, almost forty years later at age sixty-five—a body spent from the often joy-less work of sharing the joy of Christ. He made his way to Zelienople, near Pittsburgh, by rail. He bought a horse, and soon his spirits were lifted as he was "trotting happily and joyously through the forested countryside."

But it wasn't the weather alone or the view which buoyed him. Alternating between the hymnal and Bible in his pocket, he read the New Testament and sang the hymns of "my beloved Paul Gerhardt." "Many times the grace of my Savior so struck me with joy . . . that I simply had to sing aloud"[Letter from Friedrich Wyneken to Pastor Haesbaert, October 1, 1839 in *Lutherische Kirchenzei-*

tung (Nov. 15, 1838); trans. M.H.]. Wyneken found it inconceivable that America was such a beautiful land, yet people only sang in churches. "He who is no longer deeply sensible of the joy in Luther's Christmas hymns, of the jubilation in our Easter hymns, of Paul Gerhardt's 'God for us' and 'Christ for me,' should examine himself to see whether his theology is not more closely related to the Koran than to the Gospel" [Werner Elert, *Structure of Lutheranism* (Concordia, 1962), 70]. Just look at the numerous references to joy and gladness in Gerhardt's hymns! (*LSB* 334, 360, 372, 375, 438, 449, 467, 683, 724, 737, 754, 756, and 880).

The young, well-built, German pastor, Friedrich Wyneken (1810–76), founding father of the LCMS, must have been a sight and sound to behold, tramping through the wilderness, singing, baptizing, and preaching his way across Ohio, finally to Fort Wayne.

> Now rest beneath night's shadow,
> The woodland, field, and meadow;
> The world in slumber lies.
> But you, my heart, awaking
> And prayer and music making,
> Let praise to your Creator rise. (*LSB* 880)

Of course, as Wyneken himself soon experienced with a largely impoverished and divided congregation in Fort Wayne, the relationship between pastor and people is often stressed beyond joy in this vale of tears—sometimes over doctrine, sometimes over personality and weakness, sometimes when clergy or laity seek pseudo-joys. "Groaning" is inevitable, unfortunately—as inevitable as sin (2 Corinthians 5:2; Romans 8:22–27). There are a thousand ways for a pastor to seek joy, only to miss the real thing.

In his biting and deceptively humorous satire on clergy and church life, Charles Merrill Smith goads clergy into a more honest dishonesty. He lays bare the already threadbare tactics of clergy and congregant alike (but particularly clergy) to control and coerce, albeit, without appearing to do so. Tongue in cheek, he advises clergy toward the path of pseudo-joy, i.e., career success:

> We can sum up the correct philosophy of church administration by setting forth two general principles for you to follow. If you let them shape your modus operandi, success is bound to follow. They are:
>
> 1. Talk constantly about the democratic nature of the church's organizational structure.
> 2. So organize your parish that all really important decisions are made only by you.
>
> Do not try to operate on either one of these principles without the other. If you utilize only number two (as many impatient and headstrong pastors do try to operate, always with disastrous results), you will soon acquire a reputation as a dictator . . . Also if you make no attempt to conceal the fact that you really run things, you will have no one else to blame when some plan or decisions of your backfires—as sooner or later, it inevitably will.
>
> If you attempt to operate on principle number one without including principle number two (as weak and indecisive pastors frequently do), you will exhaust your energies in the endless effort to persuade pigheaded parishioners to make decisions any seeing-eye dog of average intelligence could tell at a glance are the right decisions. You will spend your waking hours in a perpetual ensnarlment of red tape [From *How to Become A Bishop Without Being Religious* by Charles Merrill Smith, copyright © 1965 by Charles Merrill Smith. Used by permission of Doubleday, A division of Random House, Inc.].

The writer to the Hebrews had no need of satire to get his hearers' attention. He had no schemes to produce pseudo-joys either. They had *"endured a hard struggle with sufferings"* (Hebrews 10:32). *"For you had compassion on those in prison, and you joyfully* [meta charas] *accepted the plundering of your property, since you knew that you yourselves had a better possession and an abiding one"* (Hebrews 10:34f.). The very fact that he addressed the issue of "obeying" leaders, indicates that the matter was a continuing problem, as it has been from the days when Jesus, the *"Great Shepherd of the Sheep"* (Hebrews 13:20), led his earthly flock of disciples (or from the days of Moses, for that matter). *"Who is the greatest in the kingdom of heaven?"* (Matthew 18:1). Or, *"Peter took him aside and began to rebuke him"* (Mark 8:32). *"How long am I to bear with you?"* (Mark 9:19).

The secret of living a good news life in a bad news world is having a pastor and increasing his joy. It is helping him to find greater joy in Christ's service and joy in you, without resorting to coercion or other pseudo-joys.

The secret of living a good news life in a bad news world is having a pastor and increasing his joy. It is helping him to find greater joy in Christ's service and joy in you, without resorting to coercion or other pseudo-joys. How does this happen?

"Obey your leaders and submit to them." What? In everything? In the color of the carpet at church? No. Let's hope the pastor is not weighing in with an apostolically authoritative word on berber versus shag! (Though there really ought be a divine *logion* on shag. . . .) The reference is to submission to the clear Word of God. *"Remember your teachers, those who spoke the word of God to you"* (Hebrews 13:7). The pastor wears a stole. He's yoked, a man under authority. He has a specific task. *"So that we may obtain this faith, the ministry of teaching the Gospel and administering the Sacraments*

is given" (Augsburg Confession V). He's been placed in an office by Christ, through your congregation, not to make you happy. He's there to bring you joy—eternal joy through faith in the eternal Word of God. *"Your words became to me a joy and the delight of my heart"* (Jeremiah 15:16). That's a pastor's goal for all of us.

But we all have the sinful nature. So when the pastor must speak the Law, we're prone to rebel, even become angry. *"If it had not been for the law, I would not have known sin"* (Romans 7:7). "Sorry, Carl! You and your girlfriend may be seventy years old, but shacking up is wrong. I don't care what the income tax ramifications are!" Can you imagine the pressure, the burden a pastor bears, being the one "who must give account" for the souls of his flock? On top of that, he has to deal with his own conscience (clearly knowing right from wrong), and face the ire of one man, one woman, a family, or even a whole community, for saying and doing what is right. No man should face this alone. But pastors often do. It can break a sensitive soul. It can sap his preaching. It can kill his prayer life. It can destroy his home life. It can drive him into loneliness and bring his visitation to a halt. It can cause him to vanish from the community.

What God gives, we receive, including the words and person of our faithful pastor. That's what faith does. When the pastor is speaking and teaching in accord with the Word of God, his authority is God's, both to call sin what it is and to absolve it (John 20:23). *"He who hears you hears me"* (Luke 10:16). This authority would seem oppressive or prone to abuse. It can be, and is, in its pseudo-forms. But as the Apology (Defense) of the Augsburg Confession states, "This passage [Hebrews 13:17] requires obedience to the Gospel. It does not establish a dominion for the bishops apart from the Gospel" (Apology XXVIII 20). Jesus certainly did not "lord it over" anyone, and Paul followed Jesus in this regard. *"Not that we lord it over your faith, but we work with you for your joy, for you stand firm in your faith"* (2 Corinthians 1:24). Peter gives pastors a specific pastoral admonition against coercion of the flock.

"Shepherd the flock of God that is among you . . . not domineering over those in your charge, but being examples to the flock" (1 Peter 5:2–3).

There is no pastor apart from the Gospel. The pastor's bottom line is Good News—joy! In fact, the word "pastor" means "shepherd." The great model for the pastor is Jesus himself. The shepherd (like God himself in the Old Testament) goes before his flock (Psalm 68:7), guides it (Psalm 23:3), leads it to pasture (Jeremiah 50:19), leads it to rest and water (Psalm 23:2), protects it with his staff (Psalm 23:4), "whistles" for them and "gathers them in" (Zechariah 10:8), carries "the lambs in his arms" (Isaiah 40:11). Jesus is the "Good Shepherd" in the New Testament. He knows each sheep and calls it by name (John 10:3, 14, 27). He seeks the lost and "lays it on his shoulders rejoicing" (Luke 15:4ff.). Joachiam Jeremias observes that "fetching sinners home is the saving office of Jesus." He notes further that "the decisive mark of the true shepherd is a readiness to give his life for the flock (John 10:11b). Jesus is *"the Shepherd and overseer of your souls"* (1 Peter 2:25), *"the great Shepherd of the sheep"* (Hebrews 13:20) and the *"Chief Shepherd"* (1 Peter 5:4). Finally, at the end of time, he will gather the flock, separate sheep and goat, and lead the sheep to eternal joy (Matthew 25:31ff.). [Joachim Jeremias *poimen* in Kittel, *Theological Dictionary of the New Testament* (Baker, 1964), 6:485ff.]. And note! Jesus is the consummate Shepherd of joy! *"These things I have spoken to you, that my joy may be in you, and that your joy may be full"* (John 15:11). Jesus is pleased when your pastor has joy in you and you in your pastor!

Your pastor is called to be like Jesus in carrying out the very office of Jesus. What an awesome, impossible, profoundly frightening vocation. The task killed Jesus. It drove Moses and Jeremiah over the edge. It landed Paul in all kinds of hot water. It threw Luther into deep psychological and spiritual funk. It brought nervous breakdown and depression to C. F. W. Walther (1811–87) and C. F. D. Wyneken (1810-76), founders of the Missouri Synod. Have you ever considered how frightening a task it is to know you must speak the Word of God, whether folks like it or not? And to do so as a sinful, emotional, fearful "maggot sack" (as Luther called himself), makes it a super-human burden. It's only possible to carry out the task with the help of Jesus and his grace (2 Timothy 1:6). Such a burden, combined with an eternally important responsibility, is enough to drive a man into loneliness and despair. But that's how Jesus became the great shepherd, and through crosses—

All Christians are called to speak the Word of God to each other, and that means speaking the Word of God (Law and Gospel) kindly to your pastor as a brother in Christ. And he needs it! The secret to joy in your pastor, and to a joyous pastor, is to love him. . . .

only through crosses—he continues to make great shepherds of fallible men (Galatians 6:14; 2 Corinthians 12:9). Through crosses, Jesus also creates sheep ready to hear the voice of their shepherd and carry each other's burdens (including the pastor's).

It was a bright, crisp morning at the Graham and Gwen Koch sheep ranch in Australia on the South Australia/Victoria border. This wonderful, humble, Lutheran couple managed several thousand sheep on several thousand acres. Graham piled us aboard his "ute" (short for "utility vehicle" . . . we call it a flatbed pickup in Iowa). As we neared the flock, a thousand skittish animals began bawling and fleeing, a sea of nervous wool. But then the scene changed in an instant. Graham began calmly, even quietly, repeating, "Hey Bob! Hey Bob!" Suddenly the flock turned toward us at once, and within a minute or two, we were in a sea of calm but bleating sheep. They were so tightly packed around the truck that I might have walked across them. The sheep knew his voice (John 10:3). It was a magic moment of profound joy and New Testament insight. I'll never ever forget it. *"But we your people, the sheep of your pasture, will give thanks to you forever; from generation to generation we will recount your praise"* (Psalm 79:13).

Paul anchored the task of the office of the ministry in the Word of God, the source of joy in this life (Jeremiah 15:16):

> Therefore I testify to you this day that I am innocent of the blood of all of you. For I did not shrink from declaring to you the whole counsel of God. Pay careful attention to yourselves and to all the flock, in which the Holy Spirit has made you overseers, to care for the church of God, which he obtained with his own blood. I know that after my departure fierce wolves will come in among you, not sparing the flock. . . . We must help the weak and remember the words of the Lord Jesus, how he himself said, "it is more blessed to give than to receive" (Acts 20:26ff.).

This passage says it all. That's why it's in the ordination rite. The pastor is a shepherd like unto Christ. He is to speak "the whole counsel of God" no matter who does or does not want to hear it (2 Timothy 4:2). He's been made your pastor by the very Holy Spirit himself (Ephesians 4:11). The flock is precious, as precious as the very blood of God. The pastor has the task of protecting the flock from wolves and false teaching (1 Timothy 5:17). And the pastor, finally, is to see that the weak and the needy are loved and cared for (Acts 6:1ff.). Through every joy and sorrow shared, pastor and people develop deep bonds of love and joy. Consider the manifold expression of frustration—yes, but overwhelming joy— that St. Paul found in his mission congregations and coworkers in Christ! And these are deeply personal references at times, of lives shared intimately, where one's weaknesses and sins are magnified by proximity! There's no support from Paul, or from Jesus for that matter, for a shepherd remaining aloof from the flock! (Romans 1:8; 16:1–16; 1 Corinthians 16:19f.).

There's the secret to joy over your pastor—that is, knowing just what he's been called to be and do. Nowhere does the New Testament say the sheep are dumb and should be silent. Not at all. All Christians are called to speak the Word of God to each other, and that means speaking the Word of God (Law and Gospel) kindly to your pastor as a brother in Christ. And he needs it! The secret to joy in your pastor, and to a joyous pastor, is to love him (*"love covers a multitude of sins"*; 1 Peter 4:8), to forgive him (*"forgive one another"*; Colossians 3:13), to care for him (Galatians 4:15), to pray for him (2 Corinthians 1:11), to defend and speak well of him, and to help him in his *"noble task"* (1 Timothy 3:1). He has an awesome responsibility, and he is *"keeping watch over your souls, as one who will have to give an account. Let him do this with joy and not with groaning, for that would be of no advantage to you"* (Hebrews 13:17).

I miss the honor of serving as a parish pastor. There is nothing quite like it. The most challenging aspect of the job is that you just can't please everybody all the time, no matter how hard you try. But the greatest honor of the office, from my perspective, is being invited into the lives of people at their very best moments and at their very worst moments. What unexcelled joy to be able to provide comfort and hope to the sick, the despondent, the dying, those struggling with addiction, or a myriad of other issues in life! What joy it was when folks came right to me with an issue that was bothering them, even when it was something I'd done to offend! What joy to baptize, to preach the Gospel, to give them the Sacrament, to lead them in worship, to marry them, and bury the dead, to care for those suffering! There was no greater joy than this service, knowing that I was forgiven my many flaws and faults, prayed for, and loved as pastor, a person. What a profound temporal and eternal joy.

Thirty-eight years after the vivacious young pastor arrived on horseback to commence his ministry in Fort Wayne, his casket was carried into St. Paul's in that same city. The body had come by train from San Francisco via St. Louis. In death, it had become all the more clear that amidst the manifold challenges of his life, his manner of living had been "an eloquent sermon in itself" (Augustine)—in some ways, not merely in spite of but because of his weaknesses. The obituary in the morning newspaper caught the note of joy over this faithful pastor:

> Eight gentlemen that had been members of St. Paul's Lutheran Church in this city more than thirty years ago, when Mr. Wyneken was its pastor, acted as pall-bearers and conveyed the corpse, which was followed by a large number of our German citizens and the professors and students of Concordia College....
>
> [Reverend Sihler preached:] "We have reasons for rejoicing, when we think of our deceased friend and venerable father in Christ.... We are created by God, and can be really happy in Him alone. Through faith in Jesus, he possessed this happiness in life, but was waiting for the life to come.... This is indeed a joyful occasion.... While here, he was indefatigable in continuing his missionary work in every direction, and gathered material for many a congregation. He cheerfully shared the hardships and poverty of his people—aye, oftentimes gave away his all to help others.... Need mention be made of his personal characteristics, his kindness towards everybody, his liberality amidst all his poverty, his sincerity and openheartedness, unfeigned humility? All know this who knew him. He had his weaknesses also, but he knew them best himself. He always renounced all dependence upon himself, upon his merits, his wisdom, and as a poor sinner, he clung and clove inseparably to Christ and His merit. With this unwavering trust, the gracious Lord whom he had served in his lifetime, had accepted him and would receive him into rest and peace and joy.... [*Fort Wayne Morning Gazette* (May 18, 1876)].

"For the Lamb in the midst of the throne will be their shepherd, and he will guide them to springs of living water, and God will wipe away every tear from their eyes" (Revelation 7:17). Oh Lord, grant your faithful shepherds increasing joy in their sacred callings, and give your people increasing joy in their earthly shepherds. We pray in the name of the Great Shepherd of the Sheep. Amen.

Study Questions:

Read or sing: "The King of Love My Shepherd Is" (*LSB* 709).

1. Who was Friedrich Wyneken, and why could he not help but sing?
2. Werner Elert rightly notes the profound joy in Paul Gerhardt's hymns. Gerhardt endured the horrific destruction of the Thirty Years' War and experienced the early death of his wife and four of his five children. Yet he knew all of life to be a gift from God. This is illustrated by the words of Paul Gerhardt in his will to his only surviving son, as narrated by Oswald Bayer: "Do good to people even if they cannot pay you back because . . . [here, the reader would expect the sentence to continue "for God will repay you . . ."]. However, Paul Gerhardt frustrates this expectation by continuing: ". . . because for what human beings cannot repay, the Creator of heaven and earth has already repaid long ago when he created you, when he gave you his only Son, and when he accepted you and received you in holy baptism as his child and heir" [Oswald Bayer, "Justification: Basis and Boundary," in *Lutheran Quarterly* (Autumn 2001), 276]. Review Gerhardt's hymns such as his evening song "Now Rest beneath Night's Shadow" (*LSB* 880) or his

great hymn on cross-bearing, "Why Should Cross and Trial Grieve Me" (*LSB* 756). How do they reflect joy in knowing the Giver of all things?

3. How does the example of Wyneken serve to encourage pastors who might be tempted to miss the real joy?

4. What do we learn about suffering from Hebrews 10:32–39?

5. By its very nature, the work of the pastor is joyful, for he is a servant of the Word. How does Jeremiah 15:16 support this truth?

6. What might rob a pastor of joy?

7. Read 2 Corinthians 1:24 and 1 Peter 5:2-3. What do these texts teach us about the joy that should mark the relationship of pastor and flock?

8. How does God "make great shepherds of fallible men"? See Galatians 6:14; 2 Corinthians 12:9.

9. What does Acts 20:26–35 tell us about the Christ-like responsibility given to pastors? Also see Ephesians 4:11, 1 Timothy 5:17, and Acts 6:1–6.

10. What is the secret to having joy over your pastor? What in Scripture speaks to the congregation loving, forgiving, and caring for its pastor? See 1 Peter 4:8; Colossians 3:13 and Galatians 4:15.

Something to Think About:

Commenting on 2 Corinthians 1:24, C. F. W. Walther says: *"Remember when you become ministers, you become helpers of the Christians' joy."*

C. F. W. WALTHER,
THE PROPER DISTINCTION BETWEEN LAW AND GOSPEL
(CONCORDIA, 1929), 407

The Joy of Giving

15

"The point is this: whoever sows sparingly will also reap sparingly, and whoever sows bountifully will also reap bountifully. Each one must give as he has decided in his heart, not reluctantly or under compulsion, for God loves a cheerful giver. And God is able to make all grace abound to you, so that having all sufficiency in all things at all times, you may abound in every good work." 2 CORINTHIANS 9:6-8

I stumbled across a surprising joy. It was at the street market in Kisumu, western Kenya, just a short walk to the shore of Lake Victoria. Twenty or thirty little street-side shops lined the way. Mind you, a "shop" is just a plastic tarp stretched across a few upright poles, with tables and boards on the ground packed with stone carvings, bowls, and trinkets.

After a couple of years visiting such markets around the world, I felt something inside of me begin to stretch and change. Suddenly, I began to see people. I became ever more intrigued and amused by the shop owners' industrious efforts, their hard- and soft-sell tactics, the way these merchants position people in their booths, the way they pull prospective buyers aside and take them into feigned confidence about a price. These merchants—barely scraping by, particularly when the tourist trade went south after 9/11—are admirable citizens in my book. I love them. My dream profession would be reaching out to them and their families, serving them in love with physical and spiritual help.

I began to see people, not carvings and curios. They are people with families to feed. And they are very adroit judges of human character. My joyous new perspective happened when the fetters on the little, constricted box in my heart suddenly broke.

Of course, there are no set prices. Locals pay a fraction of what an American will fork over, no matter how much dickering goes on. My natural inclination (and that of every one I've ever known) is to negotiate, to walk away, to "offer half," no matter what the asking price. I was just like anyone else, until the day I found joy in the old Kisumu market.

What is it about money? What is that little switch that is tripped deep within our being, right between the compassion and responsibility buttons, when money is involved? Money is a funny thing. It makes us crazy. Why does money so often render us only cheap and joyless, often under a masquerade of responsibility?

I asked how much he wanted for a beautifully carved and painted stone box, made in the shape of Africa. "Three dollars." "No, that won't do," I replied in feigned disgust. He shot back his retort, "Please sir! This is high quality!" "Nope . . . Can't do it," I repeated, a smirk emerging below my unkempt mustache. Oh, he'd end up dropping the price, but not without the requisite dance of his craft. But suddenly I threw him a curve. "I'll give you five." He was stunned; thought I was joking. I handed him the five dollars. "You work hard! You're worth it!" He was speechless. He held the money, dumbfounded, as if he hadn't earned it and didn't even know if he should take it! I laughed with delight.

This man makes $500 dollars a *year!* Why in the world would I harass him about two bucks? Two bucks will pay his kid's school fees for a week! After I spent about $25 on a half-dozen such transactions from three or four dealers, a wall came down. I began talking to them about their families, their lives, their work. I shared the Gospel of Christ. Many are already Christians. One man even ended up attending the local Lutheran church after I did business with him over the course of a couple of years (2 Corinthians 9:13). The joy I experienced, when God helped me stop worrying about paying one dollar instead of two, is a moment to treasure. It was a moment of joy.

What is it about money? What is that little switch that is tripped deep within our being, right between the compassion and responsibility buttons, when money is involved? Money is a funny thing. It makes us crazy. Why does money so often render us only cheap and joyless, often under a masquerade of responsibility? Henry Nouwen made a profound observation:

> Where is your security base? Is it in God or is it in money? It's very interesting and it's very important to realize that money is one of the greatest taboos around. Greater than sex, greater than religion. A lot of people say, "Don't talk about religion, that's my private business. Don't talk about sex." But talking about money is even harder.
>
> Money is one of the greatest taboos.... And the reason for the taboo is that money obviously has something to do with that intimate little place in your heart where you need security, and you don't want to give that away. [Henri J. M. Nouwen, *The Spirituality of Fund Raising* (Upper Room Ministries, 2004)]

"That intimate little place in your heart" is the place we reserve for our idols. *"No one can serve two masters, for either he will hate the one and love the other . . . You cannot serve God and money"* (Matthew

6:24). There's not an untainted heart in human history, not one uncondemned by this statement of Jesus. Greed is hardly the sole possession of the wealthy. I've seen an impoverished man cling to greed for what he thought was dear life. *"The love of money is the root of all kinds of evil"* (1 Timothy 6:10). The quality of greed can remain quite high no matter the quantity of money.

"Hilarity"—that special, cheerful, hopeful joy, which overlooks everything . . . and sees only Christ himself in the neighbor in need . . . is connected especially with helping the needy.

Greed makes the great sin lists of the Bible because mammon vies with God for our trust, our security, our hope. It lives in "that intimate little place in your heart," meant for God alone. *"For people will be lovers of self, lovers of money, proud, arrogant, abusive, disobedient to their parents, ungrateful, unholy, heartless, unappeasable, slanderous, without self-control, brutal, not loving good, treacherous, reckless, swollen with conceit, lovers of pleasure rather than lovers of God, having the appearance of godliness, but denying its power"* (2 Timothy 3:2–5). Among those of us with means, it's much easier to hide greed under the appearance of uprightness and reasonableness than it is other sins. *"Why this waste? For this could have been sold for a large sum and given to the poor"* (Matthew 26:8–9). Whatever does not belong to Jesus in that little place in our hearts must daily be drowned and killed and swept away. *"Oh wretched man that I am! Who will save me from this body of death?"* (Romans 7:24).

"God loves a cheerful giver" (2 Corinthians 9:7). The joyous word in the Greek is *hilaron*, from which we get "hilarity" and "hilarious." It appears but twice in the New Testament. "In both passages the freedom and authenticity of generous giving are marked by the symptom of cheerfulness" [*Theological Dictionary of the New Testa-*

ment (Baker, 1964), 3:298]. I like that. "Symptom of cheerfulness," says Bultmann, the evidence of a heart infected by Jesus! Paul, of course (quoting Proverbs 22:9), encourages the Corinthians to be generous to the saints suffering poverty and famine in Jerusalem. That's the "hilarity" the Lord loves. Hilarious joy comes another time in Romans, where Paul encourages that *"the one who does acts of mercy, [do so] with cheerfulness"* (Romans 12:8). "Hilarity"—that special, cheerful, hopeful joy, which overlooks everything (like Zacchaeus up a tree) and sees only Christ himself in the neighbor in need (Matthew 25:34ff.)—is connected especially with helping the needy. And it's willing to be wronged. "If you never want to be fooled, you will never give money" (Nouwen). But how shall I find such joy in giving? I've got a little Pharisee residing in my heart! *"The Pharisees, who were lovers of money, heard all these things, and they ridiculed him"* (Luke 16:14). But one by one, Jesus bursts the bonds of fettered hearts and drags another Pharisee kicking and screaming, through confession and absolution, to joy. The result is a cheerful generosity!

> [Jesus] entered Jericho and was passing through. And there was a man named Zacchaeus. He was a chief tax collector and was rich. And he was seeking to see who Jesus was, but on account of the crowd he could not, because he was small of stature. So he ran on ahead and climbed up into a sycamore tree to see him, for he was about to pass that way. And when Jesus came to the place, he looked up and said to him, "Zacchaeus, hurry and come down, for I must stay at your house today." So he hurried and came down and received him joyfully. And when they saw it, they all grumbled, "He has gone in to be the guest of a man who is a sinner." And Zacchaeus stood and said to the Lord, "Behold, Lord, the half of my goods I give to the poor. And if I have defrauded anyone

of anything, I restore it fourfold." And Jesus said to him,
"Today salvation has come to this house, since he also is
a son of Abraham. For the Son of Man came to seek and
to save the lost" (Luke 19:1–10).

Jesus is the *"greatest joy the human heart can experience"* (Luther,
Weimar Ausgabe, 21:293). The joy over Jesus is the *"real motive
of ethical behavior"* [Werner Elert, *Structure of Lutheranism* (Concordia, 1962), 69]. In the case of Zacchaeus the result was generous
"hilarity"—four times his former greed!

The secret of joy (being a cheerful giver) begins in the first of
five adjectives in the New Testament's great "God loves a cheerful
giver," passage. The secret is all in verse 8. All in all, the secret is
all in the "all."

"God is able," we are not able, *"to make all grace abound to you."*
God makes his plenitude of grace—grace in the word of forgiveness, grace in Holy Baptism, grace in the Sacrament, grace in the
consolation of a brother or sister in Christ —abound. Grace breaks
the fetters because it cannot be contained, it cannot be controlled.
It's stronger than all sin, all death, and all the power of the devil.
Good cheer and generosity are the products of a heart set free
from its gods. The alliteration, which follows in the Greek text, is
delightful. *"Pan-TI, PAN-to-te, PAS-an, pan."*

"So that in all things [pan-TI]"—every chance we have, every
person we meet, every gift we can give. *"The gift is acceptable"* by
grace *"not according to what one does not have, but according to what
one has"* (2 Corinthians 8:12). It's not the size of the gift that
matters, but the gift given from a heart set free. *"Truly, I say to you,
this poor widow has put in more than all those who are contributing
to the offering box. For they all contributed out of their abundance, but
she out of her poverty has put in everything she had, all she had to live
on"* (Mark 12:43–44).

"Always [*PAN-to-te*]"—on every occasion a cheerful heart set free looks for the opportunity and finds it in the smallest and most insignificant times and places. *"But when you give to the needy, do not let your left hand know what your right hand is doing, so that your giving may be in secret. And your Father who sees in secret will reward you"* (Matthew 6:4).

"Having all [*PAS-an*] sufficiency"—a cheerful heart rests in freedom and is restless in love because it knows it has sufficient means to act in love. *"Your Father knows what you need before you ask him"* (Matthew 6:8).

"You may abound in every [*PAN*] good work"—those good works are at hand in every person we meet, especially the needy. *"For I was hungry and you gave me food, I was thirsty and you gave me drink, I was a stranger and you welcomed me, I was naked and you clothed me, I was sick and you visited me, I was in prison and you came to me"* (Matthew 25:35–36).

This is the secret to joy in giving. When Jesus dwells in that "intimate little place," how can we possibly begrudge him his generosity (Matthew 20:15)? Jack, a very generous and joyous giver, once told me, "Pastor, when I started giving, I found that God blessed me beyond what I could have imagined. I cannot shovel it out faster than he brings it in." There is the secret to living a good news life in a bad news world.

"Therefore I tell you, do not be anxious about your life, what you will eat or what you will drink, nor about your body, what you will put on. Is not life more than food, and the body more than clothing? Look at the birds of the air: they neither sow nor reap nor gather into barns, and yet your heavenly Father feeds them. Are you not of more value than they? And which of you by being anxious can add a single hour to his span of life? And why are you anxious about clothing? Consider the lilies of the field, how they grow: they neither toil nor spin, yet I tell you, even Solomon in all his glory was not arrayed like one of these. But if God so clothes the grass of the field, which today is alive and tomorrow is thrown into the oven, will he not much more clothe you, O you of little faith? Therefore do not be anxious, saying, 'What shall we eat?' or 'What shall we drink?' or 'What shall we wear?' For the Gentiles seek after all these things, and your heavenly Father knows that you need them all. But seek first the kingdom of God and his righteousness, and all these things will be added to you."

"Therefore do not be anxious about tomorrow, for tomorrow will be anxious for itself. Sufficient for the day is its own trouble."

MATTHEW 6:25-34

Study Questions:

Read or sing: "Salvation Unto Us Has Come" (*LSB* 555).

1. How does Pastor Harrison's "deal" with the merchant at the Kisumu market illustrate the joy of giving?
2. What are we taught about the connection between generosity and joy in 2 Corinthians 9:6–8?
3. Why is greed a form of idolatry? See Matthew 6:24; 1 Timothy 6:10, and 2 Timothy 3:1–5.
4. What is the hilarity which Paul speaks of in 2 Corinthians 9:7? See also Proverbs 22:9 and Romans 12:8.
5. How does the story of Zacchaeus (Luke 19:1–10) illustrate Elert's point that joy over Jesus is the "real motive of ethical behavior"?
6. What does the story of the widow and her offering (see Mark 12:43–44) teach us about joyful generosity? See also 2 Corinthians 8:12.
7. How is generosity toward the neighbor in need directed to Christ Jesus? See Matthew 25:35–36.
8. Read Matthew 6:25–34. How does greed fuel anxiety? What is God's remedy for this sin?

Something to Think About:

"Once, when Luther was traveling to Jessen (a little town on the Black Elster River) to recuperate, along with Dr. Jonas, Veit Dietrich, and other table companions, though he himself did not have all that much, he gave alms to the poor there. Dr. Jonas followed his example, with the explanation: Who knows where God will provide the same for me another time! To which Luther replied with a laugh: As if your God has not provided it for you already."

OSWALD BAYER, *MARTIN LUTHER'S THEOLOGY* (EERDMANS, 2008), 96

Joy in Our Weakness

16

Then Jesus told them plainly, "Lazarus has died, and I rejoice (chairo) *..."*

JOHN 11:14

Rising like the altitude, the expectation surrounding Jesus grew as he made his way up from the Jordan—the great Good Samaritan on the Jericho road, up the western slope of the Mount of Olives, to Bethany, Bethphage, and finally Jerusalem. He had been back, way back down to the Dead Sea, where the preaching of repentance had begun a few years earlier at the Jordan (Matthew 3:1, 13; 4:17), *"where John had been baptizing"* (John 10:40). And many more *"believed in him there"* (John 10:42), even at this late hour of his earthly ministry. A very significant and purposeful event transpired over the course of the days just prior to Holy Week.

"A certain man was ill, Lazarus of Bethany, the village of Mary and her sister Martha." They knew in little Bethany that Jesus would soon be on his way to Jerusalem for the Passover of all Passovers, when the *"Lamb of God, which takes away the sin of the world"* would be slain (John 1:29). The sisters and their friends had sent messengers down the Jericho road to Jesus that Lazarus *"whom he loved"* was at death's door. He should come right away. *"So the sisters sent to him, saying, 'Lord, he whom you love is ill'"* (John 11:3). It is certain

that the sisters, and Lazarus himself, struggled with doubts about whether or not they registered sufficiently on Jesus' scale of priorities. The whole world was interested in him, after all. And they were peasants, terribly insignificant people, and from "the wrong side of the tracks" at that.

It is certain that the sisters, and Lazarus himself, struggled with doubts about whether or not they registered sufficiently on Jesus' scale of priorities. The whole world was interested in him, after all. And they were peasants, terribly insignificant people, and from "the wrong side of the tracks" at that.

It has been asserted that "Bethany" doesn't mean "House of Dates" at all, but rather "House of the Poor" (Beth Anya)—perhaps a sort of a shanty town a mile or so outside the walls of the great city for the likes of people like sister Mary (a prostitute?) who washed Jesus' feet and wiped them dry with her hair, then anointed him with myrrh (John 11:2; 12:3). Lazarus means "God helped"—another *Ezer* ("helper") description of God in a proper name. The account of the rich man and Lazarus—overwhelmingly and routinely disassociated with Lazarus, the brother of Mary and Martha—sports a number of oddities that beckon reconsideration. *"A poor man named Lazarus, covered with sores, who desired to be fed with what fell from the rich man's table. Moreover, even the dogs came and licked his sores"* (Luke 16:20–21). Though it would appear to be a parable, it's not called such in the text. I've always found it a little odd that while Paul gives us a glimpse of the portion of heaven revealed to him, and St. John as well, we are not treated to the least mention of the experience of Lazarus, who, tradition says, went on to die a second time and be buried in Cyprus. In any case, Lazarus and his sisters were precisely the kind of poor, insignificant, weak, lame, and distressed "sinners" that Jesus loved to spend time with. And this special family of believers caught his attention, probably in part because they lived in such a strategic and helpful place for him, but also because they received him with hospitality, faith, and straightforward honesty, frustration and joy (Luke 10:38ff.). The fact that Jesus had such friends and loved them so is a joyful affirmation of our life with "good friends, faithful neighbors and the like" (Small Catechism, Lord's Prayer, Fourth Petition).

The disciples were advising against the trip (John 11:8). Suffering is the antithesis of joy, after all, and Lazarus wasn't worth it. They knew what was in store for Jesus. A rabbi betrayed, tried, beaten, crucified, dead and buried, *"strength made perfect in weakness"* (2 Corinthians 12:9), was not the kind of Jesus-religion they preferred even to contemplate (Mark 8:31ff.), much less experience (Hebrews 4:15). Then Jesus threw the first shocking contradiction into the works. *"Jesus loved Martha and her sister and Lazarus. So, when he heard that Lazarus was ill, he stayed two days longer in the place where he was"* (John 11:5–6). "Jesus loved" them, yet specifically chose to delay. "Joy arises only when we despair of ourselves, and experience nothing but sadness and displeasure in ourselves" [Walther von Loewenich, *Luther's Theology of the Cross* (Augsburg, 1976), 125]. The sisters were at wit's end over Lazarus already, but Jesus drove sadness and displeasure home with a pile driver of apparent lack of concern. "Is he coming?" "Has anyone heard?" "Why isn't he coming?" "He said he's not coming?" "Why?"

He did not come. He chose to have Lazarus die because the death of this man, like his own, would result in the glory of God. *"It is for the glory of God, so that the Son of God may be glorified through it"* (John 11:4). Jesus willed that Lazarus suffer and die for good ends that were known only to himself at the time. That's the conviction Job had. *"Though he slay me, I will hope in him"* (Job 13:15). God willed that *Jesus* suffer and die for good ends that were known only to himself before the fact. *"Father, the hour has come; glorify your Son that the Son may glorify you*" (John 17:1). "*My Father, if it be possible, let this cup pass from me; nevertheless, not as I will, but as you will*" (Matthew 26:39).

Jesus waited until Lazarus had expired: "*Then Jesus told them plainly, 'Lazarus has died, and for your sake I am glad that I was not there, so that you may believe. But let us go to him'*" (John 11:14–15). The word order in the Greek is simply and shockingly this: "Lazarus has died, and I rejoice—I have a profound inner joy—so that you might believe because I was not there." Things had gone similarly with the Syrophoenician woman. "*It is not right to take the children's bread and throw it to the dogs*" (Matthew 15:26). And also with Mary, mother of Christ: "*Woman, what does this have to do with me? My hour has not yet come*" (John 2:4). Jesus rebuffs, apparently without concern, but toward supernal joy for those who persist in pleading for mercy.

"Deeply moved in his Spirit" smoothes a terribly odd and even disconcerting original text. It says, literally and strangely, "Jesus snorted [like a horse] in his spirit and was deeply shaken" (John 11:33). It reminds me of the kind of inhaling I've seen grieving loved ones do at a hundred funerals, lower jaw vibrating, lips emitting a sort of snorting sound for grief.

Jesus rejoiced because he saw through the death of Lazarus to the good ends he was preparing. Yet he certainly was not at all "happy" over the death. He certainly was not pleased to be accused of the death by grief-stricken Martha and Mary. Both sisters said to him, "*Lord, if you had been here, my brother would not have died*" (John 11:21). But unlike the account of Mary "*choosing the better part*" of sitting at Jesus' feet, and Martha "*being occupied with much serving*" (Luke 10:40), now the tables are turned. Back then it was

Martha who had said, *"Lord, do you not care?"* (Luke 10:40). Now it is Martha, not Mary, who says in faith, *"But even now I know that whatever you ask from God, God will give you"* (John 11:22). Even if Jesus had not chosen to raise her brother, he spoke one of the most comforting and oft-repeated statements in all of history—a word no doubt repeated when Lazarus died and was buried a second time, according to strong tradition, on the isle of Cyprus:

> Jesus said to her, "Your brother will rise again." Martha said to him, "I know that he will rise again in the resurrection on the last day." Jesus said to her, "I am the resurrection and the life. Whoever believes in me, though he die, yet shall he live, and everyone who lives and believes in me shall never die. Do you believe this?" She said to him, "Yes, Lord; I believe that you are the Christ, the Son of God, who is coming into the world" (John 11:23–27).

Then the account provides yet another shocking turn. Jesus himself is terribly pained by Lazarus's death. *"When Jesus saw her [Mary] weeping, and the Jews who had come with her also weeping, he was deeply moved in his spirit and greatly troubled"* (John 11:33). *"He does not willingly afflict or grieve the children of men"* (Lamentations 3:33), true. But he does afflict (2 Corinthians 12:7ff.). *"He disciplines us for our good, that we may share his holiness"* (Hebrews 12:10). *"Deeply moved in his Spirit"* smoothes a terribly odd and even disconcerting original text. It says literally and strangely, *"Jesus snorted [like a horse] in his spirit and was deeply shaken"* (John 11:33). It reminds me of the kind of inhaling I've seen grieving loved ones do at funerals, lower jaw vibrating, lips emitting a sort of snorting sound for grief. Or it may have been the kind of snorting sound of air exhaled through the lips of a closed mouth, a physical reaction to cope with intense sorrow and stress. *Jesus wept. So the Jews said,*

'*See how he loved him!*'" (John 11:35-36). He "snorted" again when he came to the tomb (v. 38). I think Jesus probably "snorted" in both ways I've noted—deep sorrow, especially pained also because the burden of the man's death had been repeatedly (three times!) placed squarely upon him. *"Could not he who opened the eyes of the blind man also have kept this man from dying?"* (John 11:37). The difficulty for Jesus was that the accusation was true. But as these Christians would soon learn through Lazarus (and through Jesus' own death and resurrection), he brings eternal supernal joy only through cross and trial.

> Then Jesus, deeply moved again, came to the tomb. It was a cave, and a stone lay against it. Jesus said, "Take away the stone." Martha, the sister of the dead man, said to him, "Lord, by this time there will be an odor, for he has been dead four days." Jesus said to her, "Did I not tell you that if you believed you would see the glory of God?" So they took away the stone. And Jesus lifted up his eyes and said, "Father, I thank you that you have heard me. I knew that you always hear me, but I said this on account of the people standing around, that they may believe that you sent me." When he had said these things, he cried out with a loud voice, "Lazarus, come out." The man who had died came out, his hands and feet bound with linen strips, and his face wrapped with a cloth. Jesus said to them, "Unbind him, and let him go" (John 11:38-44).

Lazarus's death had been incredibly purposeful. In the final chapter of his famous book, *Surprised by Joy,* C. S. Lewis quotes Augustine: "For it is one thing to see the land of peace from a wooded ridge . . . and another to tread the road that leads to it" (*Confessions, 7:21*). In this life, Jesus takes us through the valley. He even "rejoices" to know that the afflictions that he sends us are all purposeful, even though they give us great sorrow and pain (Romans 5:3ff.). That is the most profound secret of living a good news life in a bad news world. That is what sustained St. Paul and brought him to confess with deep humility and joy:

> But he [the Lord] said to me, "My grace is sufficient for you, for my power is made perfect in weakness." Therefore I will boast all the more gladly [joyously boast!] of my weaknesses, so that the power of Christ may rest upon me. For the sake of Christ, then, I am content with weaknesses, insults, hardships, persecutions, and calamities. For when I am weak, then I am strong (2 Corinthians 12:9–10).

One day, the one who commanded Lazarus, "Come out!" shall command us likewise. Until then, *we rejoice in our sufferings* (Romans 5:3).

Study Questions:

Read or sing: "Awake, My Heart, with Gladness" (*LSB* 467).

1. Read John 11:1–16. What kind of town was Bethany? How were Mary, Martha, and Lazarus the kind of people Jesus came to help? Why did the disciples advise Jesus against going to Bethany?

2. Why does Jesus delay going to Bethany until after Lazarus has died? See John 11:4, 15.

3. Read John 11:17–44. How do Mary and Martha respond to Jesus' delayed arrival? How does the Lord comfort them?

4. Read Lamentations 3:33, 2 Corinthians 12:7, and Hebrews 12:10. Taken together, what do these passages teach us about the nature of affliction in the Christian's life?

5. According to John 11:33, how does Jesus react before going to Lazarus's burial place?

6. What do the events leading up to the raising of Lazarus teach us about the way of death and resurrection for us?

7. Comment on Augustine's statement in light of Romans 5:1–5 and 2 Corinthians 12:9: "For it is one thing to see the land of peace from a wooded ridge . . . and another to tread the road that leads to it."

Something to Think About:

"The church of Peter is the church that cannot only confess, not only deny; it is the church that can also weep . . . The church of Peter is the church of divine sorrow, which leads to joy."

DIETRICH BONHOEFFER, "SERMON ON MATTHEW 16:13–18,"
PREACHED ON JULY 23, 1933 IN TRINITY CHURCH, BERLIN; *DBW* 12:480

The Joy of God's Mission

17

When they had called in the apostles, they beat them and charged them not to speak in the name of Jesus, and let them go. Then they left the presence of the council, rejoicing that they were counted worthy to suffer dishonor for the name. And every day, in the temple and from house to house, they did not cease teaching and preaching Jesus as the Christ.

ACTS 5:40–42

The old wedding photos were strewn in the rubble—all that remained of thousands of lives. The people were somber, silent, but resolute. The resolve was evident as some five hundred Indonesians worked like bees to clear the debris, dodging the bulldozers. The center of an entire city had been leveled by the aftershocks of the greatest seismic cataclysm of our era, which claimed the lives of 240,000 on the rim of the Indian Ocean. It was ghastly to behold buildings, once three and four stories high, collapsed like so many pancakes in a deadly stack. Standing in the rubble, back-up warning buzzers from the heavy equipment beeping obtrusively all about me, I wondered if there was anyone left to cherish these family treasures. The hospital was overflowing with the injured and the weak. Large portions of the facility were now unsafe and unusable. Tent cities burgeoned with thousands of refugees on the Sumatran island—a place which only days before appeared to outsiders to be an island paradise. That night, I sat alone on the beach watching the small one- and two-man craft returning with the day's catch, just as they'd done for millennia. Faced all about by such mortality, I found myself longing to learn more about a different kind of tsunami—a catechism of joy, which had struck the whole of Sumatra nearly a century and a half earlier.

Most of the people of Nias are Christian. In fact, many have studied Luther's Small Catechism, as have millions of Bataks throughout Indonesia—quite a surprise, in that it is the most populous Muslim country on earth. A tsunami of joy—no freak wave—had come to the country one hundred fifty years earlier in the person of Lutheran missionary Ludwig Nommensen (1834–1918). Because of what Christ worked through this man, millions have died . . . to death itself (Galatians 2:20).

In 1834, thirty years before the arrival of the famous missionary, two Congregational missionaries were sent by the Boston Mission Society to Sumatra (Indonesia) to proclaim the Gospel. Recent graduates of the theological seminary at Andover, Samuel Munson (b. 1804) and Henry Lyman (b. 1809) made their way to the interior, anxious to get to work in an area thus far untouched by either Islam or Christianity. Warned by Sumatrans themselves against proceeding to the Lake Toba region, they pushed on. Suddenly they were surrounded by two hundred men, attacked, murdered, and cannibalized. The gruesome martyrdom of the two men was rich fodder for recruitment by American mission societies, to be sure. The two have also been as roundly criticized as colonialists and lampooned as fools as often as Christians have praised them. But I know this much. The Batak pastors, whom I know personally, revere these men today as Christian martyrs, which they are. *"I saw under the altar the souls of those who had been slain for the word of God and for the witness they had borne"* (Revelation 6:9; see 17:6).

Some thirty years later, Lutheran Pastor Ludwig Nommensen arrived in Sumatra. He labored for several years before the first baptisms. By 1865 several tribal chiefs had converted to Christianity and brought thousands with them. By the time of Nommensen's death (1918), he had translated the Small Catechism and New Testament into Batak and established a completely indigenous church with its own pastors, constitution, and order, numbering some 180,000. With several million members today, it is one of the largest church bodies in Asia. Nommensen, with justification, has often been referred to as the greatest missionary of modern times.

The Gospel is for sinners. Indeed, Christ himself beheld his own executioners and said, *"Father forgive them. They know not what they do"* (Luke 23:34). After working in Sumatra for some time, Nommensen resolved to go deep into the jungle to find and speak the Gospel to the very individuals who had struck and murdered the missionaries.

> With several companions he found the village in the dense forest and cautiously approached. He walked straight forward to the house, where he found the man, Panggelamei, the ringleader of the murderers, a man with but one eye, about 50 or 60 years old. "My companions sat down on the earth (Nommensen later recounted), while I climbed into the house, sat down close to the old murderer and began to speak to him in a friendly way. But he sat as if he had been struck by lightning, stared at me, and moved no member, neither gave any answer to what I said. To him it seemed horrible to behold a white man before him and to hear him speak in a friendly way in his own language. For certainly, since those two had in a strange language implored him for mercy, he had not had a European so close to him.... He said that he would go and call his wife that she might prepare a meal. But as soon as he was out the door, he ran into the dense brush

and left two crying children behind him. At evening two of his sons came home, but denied their father . . . We calmly remained in the house over night, and when, on the following morning I sent his sons after him; they also hastily ran away. My feelings during the night I would not try to describe. The brethren had been murdered in the year of my birth. Of their possessions I found nothing but one of the guns." (Lorman Petersen, *The Life and Work of Missionary Ludwig Ingwer Nommensen,* n.p.)

All Christians are called to speak the Gospel in the place God has put them. The secret to living a good news life in a bad news world is knowing that the same Holy Spirit (of joy!) that animated a great missionary like Nommensen and animated the very apostles also dwells in each of us by faith in Jesus Christ. That Spirit calls some through the Church to be professional missionaries, to speak the

That night, I sat alone on the beach watching the small one- and two-man craft returning with the day's catch, just as they'd done for millennia. Faced all about by such mortality, I found myself longing to learn more about a different kind of tsunami—a catechism of joy, which had struck the whole of Sumatra nearly a century and a half earlier.

Gospel publicly to people and cultures far or near. The same Spirit gives each of us our various vocations (callings in life) and empowers us to speak the Gospel wherever he has placed us. And the Word of God, by the power of the Spirit, grants courage to fainting hearts. But joy in such a calling comes only through weakness.

Here is a crucial point—also for joy—that is very often missed in the popular accounts of extraordinary pastors and missionaries. We like the stories of the successes. We like the stories of courage and faith which conquer darkness. But when such stories are recounted, we very often fail to note that these men and women were, like all of us, deeply flawed and fallible. There is a dark side to every great story of faith. Studying the great saints of the Bible or in the history of the church, in more than just a cursory fashion, reveals joy in the midst of weaknesses and failings. The deeper the failings and weaknesses, the more profound the joy. Abraham is the great man of faith in the Gospel promise but fails miserably at key decision-making points. Moses is the great leader of God's people but has feet of clay. David slays his Goliath, but he is able to write the Psalms to comfort believers only because of his colossal failings and weaknesses. Solomon imparts the greatest wisdom in his writings, yet he is deeply flawed and even fell from the faith for a time. Similar failings could be pointed out in the case of Isaiah and Jeremiah and many of the great prophets. Peter is the "chief of the apostles," yet he not only gets the Gospel wrong while Christ was

Here is a crucial point—also for joy—that is very often missed in the popular accounts of extraordinary pastors and missionaries. We like the stories of the successes. We like the stories of courage and faith which conquer darkness. But when such stories are recounted, we very often fail to note that these men and women were, like all of us, deeply flawed and fallible. There is a dark side to every great story of faith.

with him (Mark 8:31–33) and denies Christ three times (Mark 14:66–72), but he then gets the Gospel wrong, even years after the resurrection (Galatians 2:11–14)!

Paul is able to admonish and comfort the Church in the Gospel, in spite of his deep frustrations, anger, opposition, and tribulations.

Luther is able to teach the Church the sweet Gospel of Christ in a way that had not been seen or grasped since the death of St. Paul, but that too in the midst of struggles with depression, frustration, and illness. Luther was so disappointed with the lack of the love and the fruit of the Gospel in his hometown of Wittenberg that at more than one point he had resolved never to come back. C. F. W. Walther was a genius of church organization, a master of the art of properly dividing Law and Gospel, a consummate scholar of the Church. His dogged insistence upon a kind of Lutheranism faithful to the Holy Scriptures and the Lutheran Confessions helped move virtually all of American Lutheranism in a positive direction. Yet his very insight into the Gospel was the product of a life of sorrows, loss, disappointments, breakdown, and depression. C. F. D. Wyneken was a great missionary pastor, virtually unparalleled in the history of faithful Lutheranism in the United States. He was a great and captivating preacher, an engaging personality and pastor, an indefatigable visitor and evangelist. But all of this came at the price of spending himself physically, while already the victim of childhood asthma and lifelong bouts of depression.

Nommensen climbed into Panggelamei's stilted Batak house and waited through the entire night for the old murderer to return. He never showed. He missed his tsunami of grace, his "time of visitation." Nommensen noted in his autobiography that he did not care to recount the feelings he struggled with during that horrible, dark, and fearsome night. He had the same feelings of concurrent faith and fear that every sinner/saint in the history of the Church has faced—whether in historically remarkable and dramatic moments, or in the everyday encounters of fearful interaction with that crotchety non-Christian relative or coworker. The Spirit who sustained St. Paul or Ludwig Nommensen is the same Holy Spirit who, by faith, sustains even me in my weakness. And precisely in my weaknesses, with my weaknesses, I am his witness.

For God, who said, "Let light shine out of darkness," has shone in our hearts to give the light of the knowledge of the glory of God in the face of Jesus Christ.

But we have this treasure in jars of clay, to show that the surpassing power belongs to God and not to us. We are afflicted in every way, but not crushed; perplexed, but not driven to despair; persecuted, but not forsaken; struck down, but not destroyed; always carrying in the body the death of Jesus, so that the life of Jesus may also be manifested in our bodies. For we who live are always being given over to death for Jesus' sake, so that the life of Jesus also may be manifested in our mortal flesh. So death is at work in us, but life in you.

Since we have the same spirit of faith according to what has been written, "I believed, and so I spoke," we also believe, and so we also speak, knowing that he who raised the Lord Jesus will raise us also with Jesus and bring us with you into his presence. For it is all for your sake, so that as grace extends to more and more people it may increase thanksgiving, to the glory of God (2 Corinthians 4:6–15ff.).

"Thanksgiving, to the glory of God"? That would be . . . *joy!* O Lord, grant that we too may rejoice, if only we be *"counted worthy to suffer dishonor for the name"* (Acts 5:41).

Study Questions:

Read or sing: "With High Delight Let Us Unite" (*LSB* 483).

1. Who was Ludwig Nommensen? How did he bring a "tsunami of joy" to Indonesia?
2. What had happened to the first missionaries to Indonesia?
3. What comfort does Revelation 6:9 deliver as we think of people like Munson and Lyman?
4. How does the Spirit, who animated the apostles of the New Testament and missionaries like Nommensen, also enliven us in our weakness? See 2 Corinthians 4:7–18.
5. What might we learn, not only from the "successes" of great men and women of Christian history, but also from their weaknesses and failures?

Something to Think About:

What it [the coming of Christ among us] really means, above all, is the joy of God in the world, the joy of God catching fire in humanity, which is hungry for joy. In a thousand ways people today ask, where can we find joy? Church of Christ, you alone know the answer; say it out loud: Christ, my joy."

DIETRICH BONHOEFFER, "ASCENSION DAY SERMON, 1933," *DBW* 12:468

The Joy of Everyday Life

18

Life's responsibilities and vocations should orbit about Christ in a perfectly ordered priority—like the perfect and steady circle of the planets about the sun. But they don't and never will. Remember, Kepler discovered that the planets themselves don't travel in a perfect circle, nor do they maintain a constant speed. They are hurled through space by gravity in great ellipses. They slow at the apex of the orbit, and then they gain speed falling toward the sun, only to be hurled back to the outer limits of gravity's reach. It's all-consistent, but ever in dynamic flux. So it is in our daily lives.

Never in twenty-five years of marriage had I forgotten my wife's birthday. Never. Hurricane Katrina hit the Gulf Coast on Monday, August 29, 2005. I loaded my field jacket with $50,000 in cash from LCMS World Relief and Human Care. (Remember, no electricity meant that no banks were open for weeks. The LCMS auditors never did quite understand that one . . .). A friend found a generous owner of a private jet, and I was on the ground in Baton Rouge about 72 hours after the storm hit. After several days spent in a wild flurry of activity, I was back in St. Louis on Monday, a week out from the initial devastation. The world had gone berserk. We were building, for our part, toward what eventually became (through the blood, sweat and tears of Lutherans around New Orleans and Biloxi, Mississippi) the greatest sustained operation of mercy in the history of the national church.

Two dates, two precise times during that period, are seared into my consciousness. First, at 12:00 noon (I think it was Thursday, the second week out), the phones stopped ringing off the hook at work. I vividly recall thinking, "Hey . . . they must be eating lunch again in New Orleans!"

The second moment I recall from that time was a humorous clash of vocations. We were in church. My sister-in-law had come

Then it hit me . . . If I could pull off a quick surprise birthday party, I could rescue myself from my once-in-a-quarter-century screw up. Suddenly, like a bolt of divine inspiration it came to me. I leaned over and whispered in her ear, "Honey, I think I'm gonna be sick."

from Illinois to hear our boys sing in the choir that morning. As Kathy bent over the back of the pew and hugged her sister, Teresa said, "Happy birthday!" I felt like I'd been zapped by a stun gun. "Nuts!! I forgot!" Not sure what to do, I held my fire. Then it hit me—probably about the same time as the absolution. If I could pull off a quick surprise birthday party, I could rescue myself from my once-in-a-quarter-century mess. Suddenly, like a bolt of divine inspiration, it came to me. I leaned over and whispered in her ear, "Honey, I think I'm gonna be sick." "How sick? Like throwing up?" Recalling Luther's words to "sin boldly, but believe and rejoice in Christ even more boldly" (*Luther's Works*, 48:281), I replied, "Yes, I think I'm going to throw up, but worse . . ." I feigned the sickest countenance I could conjure, looked into her merciful eyes, sighed deeply and walked out. I had, like the Syrophoenician woman with Christ, seized her at her very weakest/strongest point. My wife is deeply compassionate.

Not looking back, I sprang to life as I shot past the restroom in the back of church, and out the door to the parking lot. Within sixty seconds, I was in my car barreling toward the supermarket down the street, nervously checking my mirrors for police. In less than four minutes, I had raced through the door of the grocery store and scoped out the locale of the bakery. Another minute thirty seconds lapsed as I found a cake. Ah, divine blessing! There stood a wonderful employee, right at the counter, ready to put the "icing on the cake," so to speak. "Happy Birthday, Kathy!" While she was squeezing out the sweet greetings, I raced to the greeting cards and grabbed the first birthday card in the "wife" section. Perfect! I spied some candles, stopped for three seconds and grabbed them. Perfect! Oh . . . ice cream! Perfect!

In less than fifteen minutes, I was back in the church parking lot, goods in the trunk, and by now giggling at the prospect of actually pulling it off. I ran to the door of the church, pulse racing, chortling at the prospect of success. I stopped short of the door, took a deep breath, and forced myself to look as sick and deflated as I possibly could. I relaxed the muscles in my face and slumped my shoulders as I waited briefly for the sermon to end. As I arrived whence I'd come, I grabbed and leaned heavily on the end of the pew, slowed my still heavy breathing, and looked at my wife with everything I could possibly muster to look like the many professional beggars I'd seen for years all over the world.

"Did you throw up?" she whispered. "Ya . . ." In a stroke of luck beyond my wildest dreams, as I had run back to church, I stepped in a small puddle of white, chalky mud, and it bespeckled the top of my right shoe. I lifted my foot slightly, pointed to the providential mud and said, "The bathroom's a mess." She tensed up, whispering sternly, her beautiful blond hair jerking slightly, mirroring her determination. "You need to go. You need to get out of here—*right now!!* My sister can bring us home." I turned my face away from her. It was all I could do to keep from exploding with laughter. From the back it only looked as though my poor, ill, carcass was coughing. "O.K. honey . . . I'll hang on 'til the end of the service and go straight home."

As soon as we stood after the Benediction, I made my way to two or three groups of friends, milling about in the pews and chatting. "Listen. Kathy thinks I'm sick. Come to our house, right *now!* We're going to have a surprise birthday party for her." Resuming my death countenance once more, I weakly lifted my hand to bid my wife adieu—for all she knew it could have been the last time. "Matt, I'll stop with Teresa on the way home from church and get some Seven-Up, crackers and chicken soup." (I could have written the script myself!) She did so, but only after telling the ushers that they would need to have someone clean up one of the bathrooms.

I raced home. Our friends showed up on cue and parked away from our house. Kathy walked in with a load of groceries and remedies to begin the deathwatch. "Surprise!" And what a party we had! I regard it all as confirmation of the Lord's promise in Psalm 41:1: *"Blessed is he who considers the poor. In the day of trouble the Lord delivers him."*

The word for "church" in the New Testament is *ecclesia.* It means, literally, "called out." Christians are "called out" by Christ—out of and away from sin, death, and the devil. But this does not mean that we are called away from living real lives, or as Luther put it, should "live in a corner." To be sure, Jesus from time to time retreated to "rest for a while" (Mark 6:31) with his apostles, but quickly returned to the fray, to his sacred vocation of accomplishing our salvation. Our souls find their "rest" in Christ (Matthew 11:29), but this very spiritual peace and joy in Christ drives us back into life with both feet. If peace is joy at rest, then happily meddling in the affairs of folks around us who need us is joy in action.

The secret to living a good news life in a bad news world is coming to the deep conviction that the high callings of God, the vocations that he regards as great and marvelous, are those in which we serve folks right under our nose. "There is [according to Martin Luther] nothing more delightful and lovable on earth than one's neighbor. Love does not think about works, it finds joy in people" [Gustaf Wingren, *Luther on Vocation* (Muhlenberg, 1957), 43]. The gravitational pull of Christ draws us to himself for grace and mercy and peace and joy, and then hurls us into the world around us. For the great majority of us, that does not mean being called to serve as a missionary in Africa, or even as a pastor or deaconess or parochial

> The gravitational pull of Christ draws us to himself for grace and mercy and peace and joy, and hurls us into the world around us . . . to serve our spouse in love, to care for our children, to help our next door neighbor, to help the poor, hurting, and suffering in our church, to love our grandparents, and to serve our community.

school teacher. It means that we are driven—freely compelled (*"The love of Christ compels us"*; 2 Corinthians 5:14)—to serve our spouse in love, to care for our children, to help our next door neighbor, to help the poor, hurting, and suffering in our church, to love our grandparents, and to serve our community. And no matter what or where our calling, we are placed in a context to serve those right around us. *"Truly, I say to you, as you did it to one of the least of these my brothers, you did it to me"* (Matthew 25:40). That goes as much for changing diapers as it does for slogging to make a buck to put food on the table and pay the bills. *"For whatever does not proceed from faith is sin"* (Romans 14:23). But it is also true that whatever we do in faith is delightful and pleasing to God. We can do it with full confidence that, in Christ, all our sins are covered, and our vocations as father, mother, son, daughter, clerk, farmer, technician, teacher, fireman, or nurse are vocations in which the Lord delights with joy.

As the earth circles the sun, it maintains its own gravitational pull. It pulls along the moon, a thousand man-made "satellites," (a term first coined by Kepler), and an entire atmosphere. So it is with us. Weekly we rotate into the Divine Service. We are forgiven, strengthened, and hurled back into our lives—sometimes streaking across the sky of this dark world with a burst of joy and light; at other times with joy burning dimly under clouds of challenge and even failings. And then we pull others into the gravity of Christ, drawing them along with us to church, Bible class, and Sunday School, if at all possible.

Kepler figured out that there was a force that kept the planets revolving around the sun. Newton later labeled it "gravity." Of course, this most powerful force in the universe was there all along, though unknown for most of history. My grandmother was like that. For the first couple of decades of my life, all I saw were the garden vegetables, the "snickerdoodle" sugar cookies, the German potato salad, the seamstress at work, the wonderful greeting whenever I showed up at her door (and which I now miss so very, very much): "Well, hi, Matt!" I had no idea she was the spiritual force, the gravitational pull to Christ, the steadfast Christian who led a husband to the faith and made an upstanding Lutheran farmer out of him. She pulled along an entire clan to Christ. I don't think she went to school past the eighth grade. She never wrote anything to speak of. She wasn't known outside of her immediate community. She never made more than a small sum, sewing wedding dresses. But what a force she was, almost as quiet as gravity itself! And I'll never forget her smiling face, never. I remember when she was in the hospital dying, I told her "I'm going to study to be a pastor grandma." "*You are?!!*" she exclaimed with joy. I was tickled to learn that she had happily spread the news among the Ladies Aid at Bethel Lutheran Church in Lawton, Iowa. She knew Christ and rejoiced. And because of her, I do to.

For consider your calling, brothers: not many of you were wise according to worldly standards, not many were powerful, not many were of noble birth. But God chose what is foolish in the world to shame the wise; God chose what is weak in the world to shame the strong; God chose what is low and despised in the world, even things that are not, to bring to nothing things that are, so that no human being might boast in the presence of God. And because of him you are in Christ Jesus, who became to us wisdom from God, righteousness and sanctification and redemption, so that, as it is written, "Let the one who boasts [joyfully!], boast in the Lord."

1 CORINTHIANS 1:26–31

Study Questions:

Read or sing: "God's Own Child, I Gladly Say It" (*LSB* 594).

1. What has Christ called us from? What has he called us to?
2. How does rest in Christ enliven us for life in the world?
   See Matthew 11:29.
3. Where does "the gravitational pull of Christ" draw us?
   See 2 Corinthians 5:14.
4. How does the forgiveness of sins shape our view of vocation?
5. What is the status of all work (both good and bad) apart from
   faith? See Romans 14:23.
6. What does the story of Pastor Harrison's grandmother
   illustrate about joy in vocation?

Something to Think About:

"If we lived more fully the forgiveness of sins, such a joy would be more often our lot."

EINAR BILLING, *OUR CALLING* (FORTRESS, 1964), 33

The Joy of a Generous and Faithful Lutheranism

19

Finally, brothers, rejoice. Aim for restoration, comfort one another, agree with one another, live in peace; and the God of love and peace will be with you. Greet one another with a holy kiss. All the saints greet you. The grace of the Lord Jesus Christ and the love of God and the fellowship of the Holy Spirit be with you all. 2 CORINTHIANS 13:11-14

The Bible teems with joyous, paradoxical truths. God is three in one. God is man. God dies on a cross. The God who visits his vengeance upon trespassers has mercy only on sinners. We die to live. We live to die. The sinner is righteous. The weak are strong. Saints are sinners. Sinners are saints. Afflictions are blessings. The word of man is the Word of God. The poor are rich, and the rich poor. The first are last, the last first. Law and Gospel. It is a hallmark of faithful Lutheranism that it does not, as a matter of principle, try to resolve these paradoxes. Is it bread, or is it body? The texts simply state that it is both. If salvation is God's act alone, and faith is a result also of an eternal election to salvation (Ephesians 1), and God wants all to be saved, then why are not all saved? Must not God then have determined to condemn some from all eternity? No. The Bible says, "God wants all to be saved" (1 Timothy 2:4). Lutheranism lets the paradox stand.

Wherever the point of truth in tension is resolved, the paradox diminished or even abandoned altogether, both *faith*, i.e., belief and trust in Christ, and *"the faith delivered once for all to the saints"* (Jude 1:3; i.e., the faith which is believed), are at worst laid waste and at best labor under its weaker caricatures. So, for instance, if the tension between Law and Gospel is resolved in the direction of the Law, the result is works-righteousness, legalism, and rule-based religion with Christian trappings (Galatians 3). If the tension is loosed in the other direction, the Gospel becomes a caricature of grace in Christ, and the result is antinomianism and disregard for the created order (1 Corinthians 5–14). Grace devolves into "tolerance" and universalism, i.e., many ways to heaven. H. C. Schwan noted: "Evangelical practice is equally far removed from antinomian and from legalistic practice" [H. C. Schwan in *At Home in the House of My Fathers* (Lutheran Legacy, 2009), 487]. Thank God that the word is so powerful that it delivers its gifts, if only it's not distorted beyond recognition, by and among us (1 Corinthians 1:7).

The Church is a paradox. She is the bride of Christ, "spotless," "holy," "washed," (Ephesians 5:25–27), the "pillar and foundation of truth" (1 Timothy 3:15), the body of Christ (1 Corinthians 12:1ff.). And yet she only appears in this world hidden under the guise of poor sinners, flawed leaders, tensions, divisions, and even false teaching. This is at once both disturbing and comforting.

The maladies in the life of the twenty-first-century church, and in the Church in every age for that matter, are the result of missing the "narrow way" (Matthew 7:13–14). It is for me a paradox itself, that the "high" road of orthodoxy—right teaching and right praise—is freeing! For ortho-*dox-y* is both right *doc*-trine and right *dox*-ology (or praise). It also leaves plenty of space for us to rejoice in God-pleasing differences of gifts, emphases, practices, and even personalities.

The Church is a paradox. She is the Bride of Christ, "spotless," "holy," "washed," (Ephesians 5:25–27), the "pillar and foundation of truth" (1 Timothy 3:15), the body of Christ (1 Corinthians 12:1ff.). And yet she only appears in this world hidden under the guise of poor sinners, flawed leaders, tensions, divisions, and even false teaching. This is at once both disturbing and comforting. It is disturbing because we find ourselves in such "spotted" congregations, denominations, and Christendom. It is comforting because— despite its outward appearance, despite the fact that there have been times in the history of the church when the pure teaching of the Gospel all but disappeared from the public confession of the Church and its practice—nevertheless, the *"gates of hell shall not prevail against it"* (Matthew 16:18). The Church endures because Christ endures, and he will never let his Gospel go un-believed, until the end of time. That's worth rejoicing over, especially in the times in which we live. And there is also comfort in knowing that because the Church exists well beyond the genuine Lutheran Church, we will also find truth spoken by others. And when we do, we are free to heartily and gladly acknowledge it as such.

This is why neither people nor faith in the heart are the infallible marks of the Church's presence. Wherever the Gospel and Sacraments are—enough to bring people to true faith in the true Jesus—there is the Church (Augsburg Confession VII). Genuine Lutheranism retains this tension, the paradox of the New Testament. Nowhere is this better illustrated than in Paul's Corinthian correspondence.

Consider St. Paul's manifold and ongoing struggles with the congregation in Corinth. Despite his year-and-a-half stay with them, they were soon beset by internal division (1 Corinthians 3:10ff.), philosophical misinterpretations of Christ (1 Corinthians 1:22ff.), moral problems (1 Corinthians 5:1ff.), law suits (1 Corinthians 6:1ff.), problems with marriage (1 Corinthians 7:1ff.), numerous doctrinal problems resulting in problems with practice in worship, over food sacrificed to idols (1 Corinthians 8), over the Lord's Supper (1 Corinthians 10–11), over disregard for the weak and needy. Some were even denying the resurrection (1 Corinthians 15)! It's no small irony that, precisely because of the all the problems the apostle had to address, the Church for all ages has had such a helpful and clear apostolic teaching on all these matters and more, including joy. *We work with you for your joy, for you stand firm in your faith* (2 Corinthians 1:24).

Here is the amazing and joyous thing. In both of his letters to the

. . . Christ remains wherever, so far as and so long as, Christ and his Word are heard and to the extent that true Baptism and the Lord's Supper remain. That is the expansive joy of genuine, faithful Lutheranism. Thus, genuine Lutheranism is simply genuine Christianity. And Christianity, with all its manifold weaknesses and sins, is far broader than genuine Lutheranism.

Corinthians, Paul never regards them as anything but the precious body of Christ, his dear fellow believers. He began his long first letter of speaking truth to error, fully acknowledging this troubled bunch as Christ's own Church.

> To the church of God that is in Corinth, to those sanctified in Christ Jesus, called to be saints together with all those who in every place call upon the name of our Lord Jesus Christ, both their Lord and ours: Grace to you and peace from God our Father and the Lord Jesus Christ. I give thanks to my God always for you because of the grace of God that was given you in Christ Jesus, that in every way you were enriched in him in all speech and all knowledge—even as the testimony about Christ was confirmed among you—so that you are not

lacking in any spiritual gift, as you wait for the revealing of our Lord Jesus Christ, who will sustain you to the end, guiltless in the day of our Lord Jesus Christ. God is faithful, by whom you were called into the fellowship of his Son, Jesus Christ our Lord (1 Corinthians 1:2–9).

Paul ends the epistle on the same positive note. We know that the "holy kiss" was the sacred sign of fellowship, the "passing of the peace" before the Holy Communion. The greeting in *toto* is a fervent affirmation of church fellowship:

The churches of Asia send you greetings. Aquila and Prisca, together with the church in their house, send you hearty greetings in the Lord. All the brothers send you greetings. Greet one another with a holy kiss . . . My love be with you all in Christ Jesus (1 Corinthians 16:19–23).

In the body of these letters, joy is repeatedly spoken of, taught, and expressed. And joy is taught all the more profoundly as a result of the problems. *"If one member suffers, all suffer together; if one member is honored, all rejoice together"* (1 Corinthians 12:26). *"I wrote as I did, so that when I came I might not suffer pain from those who should have made me rejoice, for I felt sure of all of you, that my joy would be the joy of you all"* (2 Corinthians 2:3). *"I am acting with great boldness toward you; I have great pride in you; I am filled with comfort. In all our affliction, I am overflowing with joy"* (2 Corinthians 7:4). *"I rejoice, because I have perfect confidence in you"* (2 Corinthians 7:16).

The secret of living a good news life in a bad news world is knowing that despite our manifold weaknesses and sins, precisely of Christians and the Church, Christ remains wherever, so far as and so long as, Christ and his Word are heard and to the extent that true Baptism and the Lord's Supper remain. That is the expansive joy of generous, faithful Lutheranism. Thus genuine Lutheranism is simply genuine Christianity. And Christianity, with all its manifold weaknesses and sins, is far broader than genuine Lutheranism. There is a time to "separate" (Romans 16:17), and we bear the burden, knowing that the Church is found geographically and temporally far beyond the limits of churchly fellowship. But it is shocking to me how tolerant and longsuffering Paul was with his mission congregations. It's a model for us. He spoke divine truth—*"Love does not rejoice at wrongdoing, but rejoices with the truth"* (1 Corinthians 13:6)— in the most patient and loving manner, and he did so with joy even in the midst of his sorrow. And his speaking of the truth in love was blessed.

Dr. Walther took time in his enormously busy schedule as Synod president, seminary president, and head pastor of four congregations, to counsel a sensitive soul named Johann Fackler. In 1870, Fackler was a student of theology in Erlangen who was struggling over the contradiction between the Bavarian Church's orthodox confession and its heterodox practice. Walther urged him to stay. Walther confessed to the young man that he had, in fact, left his own first pastorate in Saxony to immigrate to America on unbiblical grounds. He had failed to understand the high calling conferred upon him by that congregation. In doing so, Walther admitted that he had "committed the great sin of my life." He should have come to America not as an "immigrant," but as an "exile," he told Fackler [C. F. W. Walther in *At Home in the House of My Fathers* (Lutheran Legacy, 2009), 146].

> The basis of this my counsel is that in God's Word orthodox Christians are not commanded to forsake the corrupt church, for example, in Corinth or Galatia. Instead they are to reform it [C. F. W. Walther in *At Home in the House of My Fathers* (Lutheran Legacy, 2009), 177].

That's the joy of a generous, faithful Lutheranism—generous in recognizing the Church wherever the Gospel is, and faithful in recognizing its sacred duty to be faithful to the truth of God's Word. It may be a paradox, but it's a joyous paradox, nevertheless.

> We have no doubt at all that one can find many pious, innocent people even in those churches which have up to now admittedly not come to agreement with us.
>
> PREFACE TO THE BOOK OF CONCORD, 21

Study Questions:

Read or sing: "O Morning Star, How Fair and Bright" (*LSB* 395).

1. What are some of the paradoxes we see in the Bible? Why does Lutheranism let the paradoxes stand without forcing a resolution?
2. What is antinomianism, and how is it like legalism in its distortion of the Gospel?
3. What is orthodoxy? How is it freeing?
4. Lutherans confess that the Church is the holy Bride of Christ (Ephesians 5:25–27), the pillar and foundation of truth (1 Timothy 3:15), and the body of Christ (1 Corinthians 12:1ff), yet at the same time hidden under sin and ugliness. In the light of this, how do the words of Matthew 16:18 comfort us?
5. What are the infallible marks of the Church according to the Augsburg Confession?

6. A cursory reading of 1 Corinthians indicates that the church in Corinth was beset by division, numerous doctrinal errors, abuses in worship and lack of love. Yet how does Paul address the congregation? See 1 Corinthians 1:2–9.

7. What does Paul work for at Corinth according to 2 Corinthians 1:24?

8. What is the "holy kiss" of 1 Corinthians 16:19–23?

9. How does joy show up Paul's letters to Corinth? See 1 Corinthians 12:26; 13:6; 2 Corinthians 2:3; 7:4; 7:16.

10. How does heresy rob the Church of joy? See Romans 16:17–18.

11. Why did Walther encourage young Fackler to stay in the Bavarian Church?

Something to Think About:

"Without the church, the whole world is joyless and miserable, and there is no end to hunger and thirst."

DIETRICH BONHOEFFER, "ASCENSION DAY SERMON, 1933," *DBW* 12:470

Joy—Anchor to the Future

20

Your dead shall live; their bodies shall rise. You who dwell in the dust, awake and sing for joy! For your dew is a dew of light, and the earth will give birth to the dead. ISAIAH 26:19

A young boy peered skyward at the one-hundred-foot obelisk—one hand shielding his eyes from the afternoon prairie summer sun, the other clutching the handlebar of his well-worn bicycle. His mother wouldn't appreciate his being so many blocks from home at his age. But it wouldn't be the first time (or the last) that he wouldn't tell her exactly where he'd peddled to that day. She need not worry. It was a different era, a time of innocence fading, but innocent enough still. The turmoil of the world over Vietnam, Richard Nixon, or the breakup of the Beatles barely touched his little world. The bluff on the edge of the Loess Hills afforded a view miles west over Nebraska. South Dakota was visible to the north. The mighty Missouri—channeled narrowly below with logs and debris, boiling undercurrent, and whirlpools (like the confluence of his French, Irish, German and Czech forbears)—flowed like time itself. It might as well have been the very edge of the earth. One hundred and sixty-five years earlier, it had been.

The monument, the first National Monument of the United States, was finished in 1901, some ninety years after the death of the man it commemorated. The expedition commissioned by Thomas Jefferson to explore the Louisiana Purchase had encamped a thousand yards up river from this very place. Sergeant Charles Floyd fell ill with "bilious cholic" (appendicitis) on August 19, 1804. At the last, the fine young sergeant, born in Kentucky around 1782, told Clark, "I am going away." He died—the first U.S. soldier to die west of the Mississippi—just after 2:00 p.m. on the twentieth. Clark read the funeral liturgy and recorded in his journal, "We buried him on the top of the bluff a mile below a small river to which we gave his name. He was buried with the Honors of War, much lamented." The grave was located with some difficulty one Memorial Day some ninety years later. The remains were placed in two earthen jars and interred at the base of the monument.

On that August afternoon in 1804, another man looked on with some trepidation over the journey ahead into the unknown. John Shields, who at 34 was the oldest member of the expedition and had been specifically chosen for the journey by Clark, was praised as one of "the best young woodsmen and hunters" and for his "ingenuity" as a gunsmith and more. He is most famous for the iron axe heads he forged to trade for corn while the party was camped in the dead of winter and at the mercy of the Mandan Sioux. Miraculously, Sergeant Floyd's was the only death on the journey.

> After the expedition, Shields reportedly trapped with his kinsman Daniel Boone in present-day Missouri. It is not certain what he did with his land warrant [as a reward for his service] to 320 acres in Franklin County, Missouri . . . John and Nancy Shields followed another Boone, Daniel's brother, Squire, to the area of Corydon in Harrison County, Indiana Territory, settling there in 1807. [From *The Fate of the Corps* © 2005 Yale University Press. Used with permission.]

As a boy—as oblivious to the monument's significance as I was to the wide world beyond Sioux City, Iowa—I hadn't the slightest idea that John Shields was the brother of my great, great, great, great, great grandfather, Richard Shields. Nor would I have cared. I haven't quite put my finger on just why this history should matter

I am connected to the past in a way that is meaningful to me, and because that is so—and this is somewhat hard to explain—I feel as though I can stand against the future, stand into the future, even lean into it, dash into it with courage. . . . I have an anchor, but it doesn't hold me back. It pulls me into the future.

to me at life's midpoint, but it does. Slowly, like many other things, it has become for me a piece of the puzzle of this life, put in its place; the puzzle of who I am, how I came to be, where I came to be. Suddenly I realized that the fabric of a family I'd so taken for granted, and in my worse moments wanted to forget, was woven tightly into the tapestry of America far earlier and more significantly than I had imagined. It is a source of joy—First Article creation joy, to be sure, but joy nonetheless. I am connected to the past in a way that is meaningful to me, and because that is so— and this is somewhat hard to explain—I feel as though I can stand against the future, stand into the future, even lean into it, dash into it with courage. *"I study the past, but I live for the future"* (Ronald Reagan). I have an anchor, but it doesn't hold me back. It pulls me into the future.

The secret of living a good news life in a bad news world is Jesus Christ, our eternal anchor—drawing us forward to the future, to an eternity in heaven. The foundational message of joy in the New Testament, as old as Easter itself, is the Gospel truth that, *"He is risen! He is risen indeed!"* (Luke 24:34). Christ is no anchor like the device sailors dragged through the stormy Mediterranean to slow their drift, *"fearing that they would run aground"* (Acts 27:17). Christ is no defensive device to slow the catastrophes of life. Faith is no defensive tactic to blunt the hard blows of reality. In fact, Christians have lives full of accelerated pain and difficulty, with heightened sensitivity to the cold, hard fact of sin. All of this only drives us forward to Jesus. Christ is drawing us through life, through trial and cross to be sure, but drawing us purposefully toward eternity. He does not pull us back. He draws us forward, through it all, toward himself. That's reassuring because sin, death, and the devil throw at us *"no small tempest"* (Acts 27:20). Our outlook on life is optimistic because we know that the mystery of his eternal purpose has been accomplished in the cross and empty tomb and will be fulfilled in our lives, especially when, as members of his body, our afflictions will somehow mysteriously "share in" and "fulfill" his suffering (Colossians 1:24; 1 Peter 4:13). So we lean into life, we press forward, we live in view of eternity. We dare to live purposefully, and . . . joyously.

Christ is drawing us through life, through trial and cross to be sure, but drawing us purposefully toward eternity.

The New Testament repeatedly asserts that the crucifixion and resurrection of Christ accomplished all that needed to be accomplished. There is nothing left for us to do. We only receive what has been accomplished, by faith. *"God was in Christ, reconciling the world to himself"* (2 Corinthians 5:19). *"He was delivered up for our trespasses and raised for our justification"* (Romans 4:25). Paul's teaching regarding baptism is astonishing. Baptism connects us to Jesus so that his death for sin is ours, and his resurrection is ours too (Romans 6:1ff.; 1 Peter 1:3; Titus 3:5). Baptism brings us the joy of the resurrection—Christ's and ours.

Luther has a delightful explanation of what it means that Jesus is the *"firstfruits of them that sleep"* (1 Corinthians 15:20).

> Therefore death has already been deprived of his power, and he has but few more people left to slaughter; for almost all have already passed through death, and the time is near at hand when God will present us all alive again and cast death and hell under our feet. In short, our head, yes, our back and our belly, our shoulders and legs have already passed from death, and all the hold death still has on us is by a small toe. This, too, will extricate itself soon. Therefore we who have now reached the end of the world have the defiant comfort that it will be but a little while, that we are on our last lap, and before we are aware of it, we shall all stand at Christ's side and live with him eternally (*Luther's Works*, 28:120).

What then of suffering? It is as purposeful as the very cross of Jesus, as intentional as the suffering he endured, salutary for us like the suffering and death of Jesus, whom we come to know and own firmly in trials, and in no other way (2 Corinthians 11:30). The only way we *"may know him and the power of his resurrection"* is to *"share in his sufferings, becoming like him in his death"* (Philippians 3:10). "Without the resurrection, the cross would be a cause for despair. Without the cross, the resurrection would be an escape from reality" [James Dunn, *The Theology of Paul the Apostle* (Eerdmans, 1998), 235]. In Christ I do not despair, nor do I escape from reality. I am captive to the future because Jesus has a future. I am captive to joy—my anchor to the future. That's worth *A Little Book on Joy*.

"I am overflowing with joy" (2 Corinthians 7:4).

Study Questions:

Read or sing: "Behold a Host, Arrayed in White" (*LSB* 676).

1. What does Isaiah 26:19 tell us about the joy of the resurrection?
2. How does the past pull us to the future?
3. Read Colossians 1:24 and 1 Peter 4:13–14. How do these texts cause us to "lean into life," "press forward," and "live in view of eternity"?
4. According to 2 Corinthians 5:19 and Romans 4:25, where is our future joy anchored?
5. How does Baptism bring us the joy of the resurrection? See Romans 6:1–11; 1 Peter 1:3; and Titus 3:5.
6. How do Luther's words explain 1 Corinthians 15:20?
7. How is suffering purposeful? See 2 Corinthians 11:30 and Philippians 3:10.
8. What enables Paul to confess, "I am overflowing with joy" in 2 Corinthians 7:4?

Something to Think About:

"At present we are still strangers, wandering in the time between his [Christ's] ascension and his second coming, waiting long in hope and fear. But the ransomed of the Lord shall return with singing, and everlasting joy shall be upon their heads."

DIETRICH BONHOEFFER, "ASCENSION DAY SERMON, 1933," *DBW* 12:471

"Joy's Afterword," or "Joys Afterward"

AFTERWORD
By Bernie Seter

"The congregation looks like the sunflower fields!" That is what a fellow reconciler said as we worked with a conflicted congregation. I knew exactly what he meant. In my part of the world, I can drive past miles of sunflower fields, and it is always a treat to watch as the flower heads lift up in the morning and follow the sun as if they are watching it move across the sky. I guess that's one of the reasons they are called "sunflowers." But in the late fall, when those words were spoken to me, the sunflowers are quite different. They are heavy with seeds and their heads are literally hanging down. They are colorless and dry. They have that "hang dog" expression, and so did the congregation. Weighed down with conflict—"fightings and fears within, without"—that congregation had, it seemed to me, lost the joy of their salvation. Thanksgiving was approaching, and their somber mood certainly did not match the season.

Later on, I was able to visit with members of that conflicted congregation. They had done some remediation and hard work and had come through some hard times. One of the comments that I heard many times was this: "In the midst of all the turmoil and pain, there was frustration and anxiety. And yet when it was all over, and we look back at that time and there was also . . . joy!" They couldn't define it, quantify it, or explain it, and yet in the midst of intense conflict, there was joy. I believe that it was there because, through all the mess, they sought the will of Christ. Like those seemingly lifeless sunflowers, they were bowed down because they were bearing fruit.

When my father was ill, I remember the turmoil of my life. Driving a hundred miles in one direction to be with him in the hospital, and then driving a hundred miles in the other direction to see one of my members in another hospital, and then home to worry about my Dad when I should have been sleeping. Those were hard days, and they stretched into years. Yet when I look back at that time, there is a sense of joy. I can define it: I enjoyed serving my father who had served me for years. I can quantify it: my joy was as deep and wide as my father's faith in the redeeming mercy of Jesus. I can explain it: in the midst of all those mixed emotions was a belief that this was a life well lived "in Christ," and that it was a privilege to be there at its ending.

I like the title above—"Joy's Afterword." It is meant to be the closing word on Matt's *A Little Book on Joy*. However, I think about it as "Joy's Afterward." Sometimes we don't realize the joy until it's over and a new joy is working in our life. It is, like all of the good things in our life in Christ, a gift.

Matt wrote, "So it is with joy, at least joy as a gift of the Spirit. There's no forcing it, no coercing it, no measuring it, no cooking it up. Whenever that happens, joy quickly is faked and feigned and, in fact, extinguished. . . . But joy at its best is like the kingdom of God: it "comes by itself without our prayer."

Matt kept his promise and didn't try to give us a "joy-o-meter" in this little book, or "Ten Sure-Fire Ways to Put Joy into Your Life." What he gave us was a gift because he gave us, again, the Gospel. He gave us Jesus. These perspectives on the Christ who brings joy and is joy give us again that great encouragement. When you are in the mud and your head is hanging down and things are tough, you are free to be like the early summer sunflowers. You can lift up your head and rejoice because your redemption is drawing near. You are bearing fruit because you are attached to the vine that is joy.

THE GREAT NINETY DAYS
OF JOY AFTER JOY

Daily Texts with Prayers to Gladden the Heart
From Ash Wednesday through Pentecost
(or any time)

I've found nothing so profoundly joyous as collecting and meditating upon biblical texts having to do with joy in its various forms. There is something to be said for "cognitive association" (you are what you read!), to be sure, but such texts fill the joyless void with rejoicing because the Word of God promises not to "return void" (Isaiah 55:11). *"Their arrows are like a skilled warrior who does not return empty-handed"* (Jeremiah 50:9). The texts that follow are barely a first volley. But I offer a stern warning before you proceed. You will encounter the naked, joyful Word of God. In meditating upon these little texts and prayers—that is, truly meditating—the lump of coal that is your heart (wet, cold, dank, and dark) will be subject to the blasting furnace of the Almighty God's joy in you! *"The Lord delights in you"* (Isaiah 62:4).

But take heart, others have survived it (amidst their worst trials and sorrows), and this Word of God became their greatest joy in duress. *"Your words were found, and I ate them, and your words became to me a joy and the delight of my heart"* (Jeremiah 15:16). Jeremiah wearied of holding in the Lord's wrathful message. How much more do his words apply to the Good News of Jesus! Joy! *"There is in my heart as it were a burning fire, shut up in my bones, and I am weary with holding it in, and I cannot"* (Jeremiah 20:9). Trials themselves are, as Isaiah says, *"a furnace of affliction"* (Isaiah 48:10). If you dare to find joy, step into the furnace with God's own Word. You will find—like Shadrach, Meshach, and Abednego—a Nebuchadnezzar asking, *"But I see four men unbound, walking in the midst of the fire, and they are not hurt; and the appearance of the fourth is like a son of the gods"* [i.e. the Son of God!] (Daniel 3:25).

Luther on How to Meditate on God's Word

You may certainly use the texts and prayers below at meal times with your family or as brief prayers prayed daily. You may desire, however, to actually use them to learn to meditate on the Word of God. Martin Luther wrote a little book on prayer for his barber, Peter. In it, he lays out his simple method of praying texts. It's brilliant. I call it "I.T.C.P":

Instruction
Thanksgiving
Confession
Prayer

The method anchors prayer in the texts of Scripture or the catechism but allows the Holy Spirit to prompt thoughts via the Word, which may be chased more freely by the mind at prayer. I recommend this method for the ninety days. It requires a time of solitude, and intentionality. It will also require a period of preparation—perhaps following a brief order for prayer like that found on pages 294–298 of *Lutheran Service Book* (Concordia, 2006) or the inside front cover of *The Lutheran Study Bible* (Concordia, 2009).

Luther gave Peter the barber some examples of how he prayed, but:

You should also know that I do not want you to recite all these words in your prayer. That would make it nothing but idle chatter and prattle, read word for word out of a book as were the rosaries by the laity and the prayers of the priests and monks. Rather do I want your heart to be stirred and guided concerning the thoughts, which ought to be comprehended in the Lord's Prayer. These thoughts may be expressed, if your heart is rightly warmed and inclined toward prayer, in many different ways and with more words or fewer. I do not bind myself to such words or syllables, but say my prayers in one fashion today, in another tomorrow, depending upon my mood and feeling. I stay however, as nearly as I can, with the same general thoughts and ideas. It may happen occasionally that I may get lost among so many ideas in one petition that I forego the other six. If such an abundance of good thoughts comes to us we ought to disregard the other petitions, make room for such thoughts, listen in silence, and under no circumstances obstruct them. The Holy Spirit himself preaches here, and one word of his sermon is far better than a thousand of our prayers. Many times I have learned more from one prayer than I might have learned from much reading and speculation . . . (*Luther's Works*, 43:198).

Luther explains his method, using the Ten Commandments:

I think of each commandment as, first, instruction, which is really what it is intended to be, and consider what the Lord God demands of me so earnestly. Second, I turn it into a *thanksgiving;* third, a *confession;* and fourth, a *prayer.* I do so in thoughts or words such as these: "I am the Lord your God, etc. You shall have no other gods before me," etc. Here I earnestly consider that God expects and teaches me to trust him sincerely in all things and that it is his most earnest purpose to be my God. I must think of him in this way at the risk of losing eternal salvation. My heart must not build upon anything else or trust in any other thing, be it wealth, prestige, wisdom, might, piety, or anything else.

Second, I give thanks for his infinite compassion by which he has come to me in such a fatherly way and, unasked, unbidden, and unmerited, has offered to be my God, to care for me, and to be my comfort, guardian, help, and strength in every time of need. We poor mortals have sought so many gods and would have to seek them still if he did not enable us to hear him openly tell us in our own language that he intends to be our God. How could we ever—in all eternity—thank him enough!

Third, I confess and acknowledge my great sin and ingratitude for having so shamefully despised such sublime teachings and such a precious gift throughout my whole life, and for having fearfully provoked his wrath by countless acts of idolatry. I repent of these and ask for his grace.

Fourth, I pray and say: "O my God and Lord, help me by thy grace to learn and understand thy commandments more fully every day and to live by them in sincere confidence. Preserve my heart so that I shall never again become forgetful and ungrateful, that I may never seek after other gods or other consolation on earth or in any creature, but cling truly and solely to thee, my only God. Amen, dear Lord God and Father. Amen" (*Luther's Works* 43:200).

A Sad Brightness, and a Bright Sadness

"Eh, what muddleheads you peoples are! How do you keep Lent?" (Dostoyevsky, *The Brothers Karamazov*). We are "muddleheads," indeed, when we fail to see that Lent is also a time of joy. I am no fan of Eastern Orthodoxy but heartily concur with Alexander Schmemann's description of Lent as

> "Sad brightness": the sadness of my exile, of the waste I have made of my life; the brightness of God's presence and forgiveness, the joy of the recovered desire for God, the peace of the recovered home. Such is the climate of Lenten worship; such is its first and general impact on my soul [Schmemann, *Great Lent* (St. Vladimir, 1974), 33].

And so, beginning with Ash Wednesday, I have added the forty days of Lent to the journey of joy. By the second century, the forty day period of preparation for baptism on Holy Saturday was well established in many places in the Church. The "fasting" of Lent did not include the Sundays which were "in" but not "of" Lent, and so I have not numbered them below. From the festival of the Resurrection to Pentecost are fifty days, long called "Fifty Days of Joy" by the Church, and also the Lutheran Church [Hermann Sasse, "Fifty Days of Joy," *Lutheran Herald* (April 8, 1961)]. The ninety days include two distinct periods. The first, forty days of "sad brightness" (Lent). The second, fifty days of Eastertide, a "bright sadness"—that is, a life facing sin, death, and the devil, but with an unquenchable resurrection joy. Thus, Ninety Days of Joy after Joy.

For the weeks prior to Easter, I have generally ordered the texts according to a regular, recurring, daily theme (common for Lent), and connected also to the theme of the previous Sunday if possible. For the weeks after Easter, I have allowed the texts to follow the themes and order of the Small Catechism, except for the Sundays.

Sunday—Joyous theme of the week
Monday—Joy in the Old Testament
Tuesday—Joy in caring for the needy
Wednesday—Joy in the Gospels
Thursday—Joy in Epistles, amidst affliction etc.
Friday—Joy in God's gifts in this world
Saturday—Joy in repentance

Prepare to meditate. Find a quiet spot. A comfortable kneeler focuses the attention well, but you will probably find yourself at a table, a desk, or a favorite easy chair. Take a few deep, clearing breaths, and continue to breath deeply. Recite the Lord's Prayer. Clear your mind. Pray for clarity of mind and a receptive heart. Now read the text and prayer.

> 1. Ash Wednesday: *Blow a trumpet in Zion; sound an alarm on my holy mountain! Let all the inhabitants of the land tremble, for the day of the Lord is coming; it is near . . . "Yet even now," declares the Lord, "return to me with all your heart, with fasting, with weeping, and with mourning; and rend your hearts and not your garments." Return to the Lord your God, for he is gracious and merciful, slow to anger, and abounding in steadfast love; and he relents over disaster. "Fear not, O land; be glad and rejoice, for the Lord has done great things! . . . Be glad, O children of Zion, and rejoice in the Lord your God . . ."* (Joel 2:1, 12–13, 21, 23).

Read it again, slowly. What words are beginning to jump at you? What words trouble you? Encourage you? Disturb you? Comfort you? *What does this text teach you?* Possibilities abound: true repentance, God's seriousness over repentance, he wants the heart. God is merciful and gracious. He acts for our benefit. We need not fear. *What do we have to be thankful for in this text?* Many of the same things about which he instructs us, to be sure. I'm thankful that the Lord desires us to "be glad and rejoice." *What can we confess?* Thankless hearts, lack of repentance, false repentance, rejection of the Lord's steadfast love. *Now pray.*

> *Instruction:* O Lord, you teach us here that you desire true repentance and sorrow over sin, and that you are merciful and slow to anger. You also desire our joy in you.

> *Thanksgiving:* I thank you for your mercies, for your call to repentance, for your patience with me, for your mercy, for your steadfast love.

> *Confession:* I confess my many sins, my lack of repentance, my insincerity, my failure to follow through, secret sins of weakness, and especially my great lack of joy.

> *Prayer:* Righteous and Just Judge, you know the hearts of all. Help me, I pray, in this time of repentance, to acknowledge my sinfulness with true sorrow. Forgive my many failings and faults, and grant me increasing joy in your eternal mercies; through Jesus Christ our Lord. Amen.

That's "I.T.C.P."—*Instruction, Thanksgiving, Confession, Prayer.* As you practice it daily, it will become second nature and a great blessing for your meditation and prayer. You may certainly read the texts with your family at the table, with your women's/men's group, or by yourself, even without using Luther's method. You can also use Luther's method as a catechetical tool with your family or others. In any case, prepare for "joy after joy."

2. Thursday: *Your [joyful] boasting is not good. Do you not know that a little leaven leavens the whole lump? Cleanse out the old leaven that you may be a new lump, as you really are unleavened. For Christ, our Passover lamb, has been sacrificed. Let us therefore celebrate the festival, not with the old leaven, the leaven of malice and evil, but with the unleavened bread of sincerity and truth* (1 Corinthians 5:6–8). Dear Jesus, only Savior, I confess my malice, lack of charity toward the needy, my cold response to your Word, my lack of love and begrudging service to my family. Grant me true repentance and deep sorrow over my sin that I may rejoice and find joy in your resurrection. Amen.

3. Friday: *Your words were found, and I ate them, and your words became to me a joy and the delight of my heart, for I am called by your name, O Lord, God of hosts* (Jeremiah 15:16). Oh Lord God, you set the table, a joyful feast of your Word. May I devour it with delight and find joy in all its delicacies, through Jesus Christ, by whose name I'm named "Christian." Amen.

4. Saturday: *All who pass along the way clap their hands at you; they hiss and wag their heads at the daughter of Jerusalem: "Is this the city that was called the perfection of beauty, the joy of all the earth?"* (Lamentations 2:15). Lord, you are pleased to be believed upon by your Holy Church, which is nothing but the totality of dreadful sinners, often joyless dolts, who nevertheless cling to you by faith. In you we are "the perfection of beauty." Grant that we may be truly, "the joy of all the earth." Amen.

Week of Lent 1 (Invocavit)

Sunday: *When he calls to me, I will answer him; I will be with him in trouble.* Psalm 91:15. *And when he comes home, he calls together his friends and his neighbors, saying to them, "Rejoice with me, for I have found my sheep that was lost"* (Luke 15:6). O Jesus, my Joy, you are my Good Shepherd, you take delight in calling me by name, finding me when lost, and celebrating my return. Grant that I might have a heart like yours for others, and rejoice likewise. Amen.

5. Monday: *Happy are you, O Israel! Who is like you, a people saved by the Lord, the shield of your help, and the sword of your triumph! Your enemies shall come fawning to you, and you shall tread upon their backs* (Deuteronomy 33:29). Heavenly Father, in Christ we "tread upon the backs" of our enemies—sin, death and the devil. Grant unto me a restoration of happiness over your salvation; through Jesus, Amen.

6. Tuesday: *The meek shall obtain fresh joy in the Lord, and the poor among mankind shall exult in the Holy One of Israel* (Isaiah 29:19). Make me, O Lord, a source of fresh joy in the Lord to the meek and poor. Turn my selfish, greedy, joyless heart, and make me a "joyful giver." May the poor exult in you because of your gifts to them through me. Amen.

7. Wednesday: *Elizabeth will bear you a son, and you shall call his name John. And you will have joy and gladness, and many will rejoice at his birth, for he will be great before the Lord. . . . And he will turn many of the children of Israel to the Lord their God* (Luke 1:13–16). Your Law is harsh, O righteous Judge, but sweet are your mercies in Christ. Strike me with your Law, through the words of your prophet John the Baptizer, that I may ever repent and find joy in the presence of the Kingdom; through Jesus Christ, Amen.

8. Thursday: *Blessed be the God and Father of our Lord Jesus Christ! According to his great mercy, he has caused us to be born again to a living hope through the resurrection of Jesus Christ from the dead . . . In this you rejoice, though now for a little while, if necessary, you have been grieved by various trial*s (1 Peter 1:3–6). Jesus, my hope and crown, I thank you also for the crosses and afflictions you wisely send to me. They cause me to look forward in living hope to your resurrection, which is the guarantee of my own. Please help me to rejoice in this "little while" of trials and difficulties. Amen.

9. Friday: *Let those who delight in my righteousness shout for joy and be glad and say evermore, "Great is the Lord, who delights in the welfare of his servant!"* (Psalm 35:27). O Lord, your Word tells me again and again that you delight in me. I don't deserve it. And that is your very delight. Increase my joy in your joy in me! Through Jesus Christ, my Lord. Amen.

10. Saturday: *Let me hear joy and gladness; let the bones that you have broken rejoice* (Psalm 51:8). Gracious God, my sins are many. My conscience is unclean. My transgressions nag at me and cause me anxiety. I have sinned against my family, my coworkers, my fellow Christians and you. My bones are broken. Forgive me my many sins. As I go to church tomorrow, let me hear joy and gladness in the absolution of all my sins. In Jesus, Amen.

Week of Lent 2 (Reminiscere)

Sunday: *Remember your mercy, O Lord, and your steadfast love, for they have been from of old* (Psalm 25:6). Like the Syrophoenician woman, O Lord, I'm holding you to your merciful Word. "Even the dogs eat what falls from the master's table, Lord." A few crumbs of your blessed mercy shall sustain me in eternal joy. Amen.

11. Monday: *You make known to me the path of life; in your presence there is fullness of joy; at your right hand are pleasures forevermore* (Psalm 16:11). Lord, I want nothing more than your path of life, your presence, and your fullness of joy. Yet "the good that I would I do not." Forgive me. Renew me. Restore me. Preserve me in "the joy of your salvation." I plead it in the name of Jesus, who is seated at your right hand. Amen.

12. Tuesday: *"For he [an evil man] did not remember to show kindness, but pursued the poor and needy and the brokenhearted, to put them to death. . . . Let them curse, but you will bless! They arise and are put to shame, but your servant will be glad! . . . With my mouth I will give great thanks to the Lord; I will praise him in the midst of the throng* (Psalm 109:16ff., 30). O Lord, Father of all mercies, you delight in kind-

ness shown to the needy and sorrowful. Give me a heart after your own and cause me to be glad. I give you thanks! Amen!

13. Wednesday: *When a woman is giving birth, she has sorrow because her hour has come, but when she has delivered the baby, she no longer remembers the anguish, for joy that a human being has been born into the world. So also you have sorrow now, but I will see you again, and your hearts will rejoice, and no one will take your joy from you* (John 16:21–22). Jesus, you consoled your blessed apostles in the dark hour of your passion. Console me now and in all times of trial and trouble. Do not let my spark of joy in you be snuffed out, but through every trial and affliction, cause it to burn more brightly until I see you face to face. Amen.

14. Thursday: *As I remember your tears, I long to see you, that I may be filled with joy* (2 Timothy 1:4). Good Shepherd, through your blessed apostle and martyr, St. Paul, you teach us how good and right it is for pastors to love their people, and for the flock to love its shepherd. Fill your Church with such love and joy—now, today, here. Amen.

15. Friday: *For he will not much remember the days of his life because God keeps him occupied with joy in his heart* (Ecclesiastes 5:20). My Blessed Maker and Redeemer, give me joy in my inmost being—joy in you, joy in your Gospel, joy in your forgiveness, joy in your love, joy in your Sacraments, joy in your Church. Occupy my heart, in the name of Jesus. Amen.

16. Saturday: *So if a person lives many years, let him rejoice in them all; but let him remember that the days of darkness will be many. All that comes is vanity* (Ecclesiastes 11:8). In times of darkness, gracious Lord, cause me to recall your merciful promises. Help me to remember that you send afflictions as a loving father chastens a child. Purify me, O God; only take not the joy of your salvation from me. Amen.

Week of Lent 3 (Oculi)

Sunday: *My eyes are ever toward the Lord, for he will pluck my feet out of the net. Turn to me and be gracious to me, for I am lonely and afflicted* (Psalm 25:15–16). *Now the people of Beth-shemesh were reaping their wheat harvest in the valley. And when they lifted up their eyes and saw the ark, they rejoiced to see it* (1 Samuel 6:13). Lord of all consolation, I am Ichabod; I feel as though your glory has departed from my life. Cause me to rejoice even in my sufferings. Strengthen my confidence under the cross in your cross. Cause me to lift my eyes to you in your blessed Word and Sacrament, and to rejoice, you who live and reign with the Son and the Holy Spirit. Amen.

17. Monday: *The precepts of the Lord are right, rejoicing the heart; the commandment of the Lord is pure, enlightening the eyes* (Psalm 19:8). Your perfect Law, O Lord, reveals my horrid imperfection. By your Law, drive me to your Son Jesus Christ and his perfect sacrifice, that forgiven and renewed, I may rejoice in your commands. Amen.

18. Tuesday: *Then the eyes of the blind shall be opened, and the ears of the deaf unstopped; then shall the lame man leap like a deer, and the tongue of the mute sing for joy . . . And the ransomed of the Lord shall return and come to Zion with singing; everlasting joy shall be upon their heads; they shall obtain gladness and joy, and sorrow and sighing shall flee away* (Isaiah 35:5, 6, 10). O Jesus, hope of all the afflicted, the prophets foretold your great love for those in need, those who are afflicted and ill, downtrodden and imperfect. The joy of the weak, the sick, the disabled, the elderly and the oppressed is ever a sign of your kingdom. Preserve me in your kingdom of mercy, and cause my heart to burn with joyful compassion for all. Amen.

19. Wednesday: *Then turning to the disciples he said privately, "Blessed [happy!] are the eyes that see what you see!"* (Luke 10:23). In the Holy Gospels, we see you, Jesus! We behold the mysteries of eternity! We are blessed to see the depth of your love and compassion in your cross. We see you through the eyes and ears of the

blessed Evangelists! And we are blessed and happy in you! Amen.

20. Thursday: *The eye cannot say to the hand, "I have no need of you," nor again the head to the feet, "I have no need of you." . . . If one member suffers, all suffer together; if one member is honored, all rejoice together* (1 Corinthians 12:21, 26). If it be necessary, O God, if it be necessary to increase my suffering that I learn to treasure the gift of your body, the Church, so be it. Only grant that I learn to suffer with and to help others, and that I may rejoice, together with all your saints, in you; through Jesus Christ. Amen.

21. Friday: *You have captivated my heart, my sister, my bride; you have captivated my heart with one glance of your eyes, with one jewel of your necklace* (Song of Solomon 4:9). O Blessed Jesus, sender of all good gifts, you have given me my spouse. Tender love and affection is most pleasing to you. Cause me to find delight in her/him, that as husband and wife, we may live chastely and joyfully together, through every joy and sorrow shared. Amen.

22. Saturday: *Is not the food cut off before our eyes, joy and gladness from the house of our God?* (Joel 1:16). Righteous God, Just Judge of all the living and the dead, cause your Law to strike unrepentant hearts—beginning with my own—that "cut off," I be left seeking only you. And tomorrow in church, restore to me joy and gladness in your house; through Jesus Christ, my only hope. Amen.

Week of Lent 4 (Laetare)

Sunday: *I was glad when they said to me, "Let us go to the house of the Lord!"* (Psalm 122:1). In the gathering of your Church this day, I bless your name, rejoicing in your mercies. Cause my congregation to grow in grace. Give my pastor the strength and faith he needs daily to face many challenges. Cause a love for your word to burn deeply in the hearts of your people. Give me a passion for the lost and erring, the lonely and the shut-in, O Jesus, Blessed Savior. Amen.

23. Monday: *And Hannah prayed and said, "My heart exults in the*

Lord; my strength is exalted in the Lord. My mouth derides my enemies, because I rejoice in your salvation" (1 Samuel 2:1). Like Hannah, I offer to you, O Lord, the favorite son of my soul—my pride, my bitterness toward others, my thankless joyless heart. Cause my enemies—sin, death and the devil—to flee before you, that I may rejoice in your salvation. In Jesus, Amen.

24. Tuesday: *And you shall rejoice before the Lord your God, you and your son and your daughter, your male servant and your female servant, the Levite who is within your towns, the sojourner, the fatherless, and the widow who are among you, at the place that the Lord your God will choose, to make his name dwell there* (Deuteronomy 16:11). Most Holy Trinity, you dwell in your Church by your mighty Word, enfleshed in Jesus. By the eternal Word of all joy and mercy, cause me to love my neighbor, to be generous to the needy. Grant that my congregation and my pastor overflow with love for the least of these my brethren. May it please you to use me as a vessel of your mercy—now, today. Amen.

25. Wednesday: *Nevertheless, do not rejoice in this, that the spirits are subject to you, but rejoice that your names are written in heaven* (Luke 10:20). O Christ, you told the apostles "you did not choose me, but I chose you" (John 15:16). Give me joy in your gracious election to life, and deep humility in all matters in this life. May I be known in this life only as a sinner forgiven. Amen.

26. Thursday: *Rejoice in hope, be patient in tribulation, be constant in prayer* (Romans 12:12). Lord God, Heavenly Father, through tribulation you produce patience and hope. Grant that I not fall into despair and doubt regarding your mercies or purposeful actions in my life. Increase my life of prayer. Cause me to rejoice in all humility before you; through Jesus Christ, my only hope. Amen.

27. Friday: *I rejoice at the coming of Stephanas and Fortunatus and Achaicus, because they have made up for your absence* . . . (1 Corinthians 16:7). Through your faithful Apostle Paul, Lord, you have repeatedly shown that you delight in Christian friends who love

and cherish one another in joy. Grant that this day I may be a joy to a brother or sister in Christ, and especially to my pastor. Grant him blessed joy in me, and in all his flock this day. Amen.

28. Saturday: *And I wrote as I did, so that when I came I might not suffer pain from those who should have made me rejoice, for I felt sure of all of you, that my joy would be the joy of you all* (2 Corinthians 2:3). Lord of the Church, give my pastor courage to speak the Law to sin. Grant me and all my congregation humility and repentance. Restore to us all the joy in which you delight. I plead it in Jesus' name and for his sake. Amen.

Week of Lent 5 (Judica)

Sunday: *Vindicate me, O God, and defend my cause against an ungodly people, from the deceitful and unjust man deliver me! ... Then I will go to the altar of God, to God my exceeding joy, and I will praise you with the lyre, O God, my God* (Psalm 43:1, 4). Today, Lord, I thank you for the musicians who will be served by your Word and Sacrament, and who will in turn serve you and your Church with their talents. Grant all of us exceeding joy before your altar, and in the gift of your body and blood. Strengthen us all with your forgiveness, and vindicate us by that forgiveness in the face of an accusing world; through Christ. Amen.

29. Monday: *Let your priests be clothed with righteousness, and let your saints shout for joy* (Psalm 132:9). In your wondrous Church, O Lord, we are all priests. We present our hearts' lament to you, and we offer the sacrifice of prayer, praise, and thanksgiving. We offer the sweet smelling sacrifice of love to our neighbor. Only continue to cover us with your righteousness, O Christ, that we may be your saints and shout for joy! Amen.

30. Tuesday: *Then he said to them, "Go your way. Eat the fat and drink sweet wine and send portions to anyone who has nothing ready, for this day is holy to our Lord. And do not be grieved, for the joy of the Lord is your strength"* (Nehemiah 8:10). O Jesus, restore your

Church as you once restored Jerusalem! May we feast on your holy Word and find our delight in you alone. And give us zeal to share such portions with "anyone who has nothing," in word and deed. Amen.

31. Wednesday: *"Zacchaeus, hurry and come down, for I must stay at your house today." So he hurried and came down and received him joyfully. . . . "Behold, Lord, the half of my goods I give to the poor. And if I have defrauded anyone of anything, I restore it fourfold." And Jesus said to him, "Today salvation has come to this house, since he also is a son of Abraham. For the Son of Man came to seek and to save the lost"* (Luke 19:5ff.). You, O Lord, are the great consolation of the poor and needy. Give me the zeal and sheer joy of Zacchaeus to see you in your Church in time, and in eternity in heaven. Give me the humility to amend my sinful life and make fourfold restoration when I sin against others. Amen.

32. Thursday: *For the kingdom of God is not a matter of eating and drinking but of righteousness and peace and joy in the Holy Spirit* (Romans 14:17). Grant, gracious God, that I delight in and find joy in my Christian freedom, for all good gifts of food and drink come from you and give joy to my heart (Psalm 104). But help me always to use this freedom to advance your righteousness and for peace and joy in the Spirit, for the sake of your kingdom. Amen.

33. Friday: *Then Jesus told them plainly, "Lazarus has died, and for your sake I am glad that I was not there, so that you may believe. But let us go to him." So Thomas, called the Twin, said to his fellow disciples, "Let us also go, that we may die with him"* (John 11:14–16). Help me, Lord, to recognize that you use every means, even death, that I may look to you as my only hope. And when I am sad because of cross and affliction, you are acting for my joy. Only give me the strength to die joyously with you. Amen.

34. Saturday: *You meet him who joyfully works righteousness, those who remember you in your ways. Behold, you were angry, and we sinned; in our sins we have been a long time, and shall we be saved?*

(Isaiah 64:5). Triune God, Fire of Righteousness, turn your wrath from me, for I am a great sinner. Grant me forgiveness by your mercy in Christ, and cause me joyfully to work righteousness in the lives of those around me this day. Amen.

Holy Week (Palmarum)

Palm Sunday—Jesus Enters Jerusalem: *Rejoice greatly, O daughter of Zion! Shout aloud, O daughter of Jerusalem! Behold, your king is coming to you; righteous and having salvation is he, humble and mounted on a donkey, on a colt, the foal of a donkey* (Zechariah 9:9). I am completely unworthy of your presence. Like your people of old, I sin grievously in thought, word, and deed. And yet you come, my King, righteous and having salvation for me. I rejoice greatly today, with all of Zion! Amen.

35. Monday of Holy Week—Jesus Clears the Temple: *"I will bring [them] to my holy mountain, and make them joyful in my house of prayer; their burnt offerings and their sacrifices will be accepted on my altar; for my house shall be called a house of prayer for all peoples"* (Isaiah 56:7). O burning Fire of Righteousness, by my own greed and selfishness, I have established a den of thieves in the temple of my own heart. I am weak! I am lost! Cleanse the temple, Lord! Turn the tables! Forgive my many sins that I may humbly offer you the sacrifice of a broken heart with joy, and joyfully pray to you; through Jesus. Amen.

36. Tuesday of Holy Week—Day of Controversy and Parables: *His master said to him, "Well done, good and faithful servant. You have been faithful over a little; I will set you over much. Enter into the joy of your master"* (Matthew 25:23). How many times I have wasted my "talents." How many times have I not been faithful in the little things. Forgive, restore, renew. In Christ I know that I shall nevertheless hear one day, "Enter the joy." Grant it by your mercy, O Savior. Amen.

37. Wednesday of Holy Week—Judas Conspires with the

Authorities: *Then Satan entered into Judas called Iscariot, who was of the number of the twelve. He went away and conferred with the chief priests and officers how he might betray him to them. And they were glad, and agreed to give him money* (Luke 22:3–5). How often, Lord, have I been only too happy to betray you, even plotting against you. For you said, "Whatever you have done to the least of these, you have done it to me." At least Judas did it for money. I most often do it for nothing but vainglory. Forgive me my wretched sins. I gladly die with you. Plunge me into your death by my baptism that I may rejoice again. Amen.

38. Maundy Thursday—Jesus Is Betrayed: *And joy and gladness are taken away from the fruitful field, and in the vineyards no songs are sung, no cheers are raised; no treader treads out wine in the presses; I have put an end to the shouting* (Isaiah 16:10). On Olivet you prayed "Not my will but yours be done." Lord, let me die with you that I may live with you for eternity. Let not my will be done, but yours. Put an end to all my boasting which is not in you and your cross. Help me, Jesus, that I may rejoice again. Amen.

39. Good Friday—Jesus Is Crucified: *My God, my God, why have you forsaken me? Why are you so far from saving me, from the words of my groaning? . . . I am a worm and not a man, scorned by mankind and despised by the people. All who see me mock me; they make mouths at me; they wag their heads; he trusts in the Lord; let him deliver him; let him rescue him, for he delights in him!*" (Psalm 22:1, 6–8). O Dying Christ, I am loathe to contemplate the death of God in the flesh on the cross, the wrath of the Father poured out on you for me. You are my sin. You are my thanklessness. You are my joylessness. You are my hopelessness. The Father made you who "knew no sin to be sin for us" (2 Corinthians 5:21). O Source of unending wonder and joy, I shall joyfully "proclaim your righteousness to a people yet unborn, that you have done it" (Psalm 22:31). Amen.

40. Holy Saturday—Jesus in the Grave: *I have set the Lord always before me; because he is at my right hand, I shall not be shaken. Therefore my heart is glad, and my whole being rejoices; my flesh also dwells secure. For you will not abandon my soul to Sheol, or let your holy one see corruption. You make known to me the path of life; in your presence there is fullness of joy; at your right hand are pleasures forevermore* (Psalm 16:8–11). I shall die, but not even death shall not steal my joy, O Christ. For you have gone before me into the tomb. Because of you, death shall be for me but like a brief nap from which I shall awaken refreshed, to rejoice in eternity. Amen.

Week of Easter

41. Easter Sunday: *But the angel said to the women, "Do not be afraid, for I know that you seek Jesus who was crucified. He is not here, for he has risen, as he said. Come, see the place where he lay. Then go quickly and tell his disciples that he has risen from the dead, and behold, he is going before you to Galilee; there you will see him. See, I have told you." So they departed quickly from the tomb with fear and great joy, and ran to tell his disciples. And behold, Jesus met them and said, "Greetings!" And they came up and took hold of his feet and worshiped him. Then Jesus said to them, "Do not be afraid; go and tell my brothers to go to Galilee, and there they will see me"* (Matthew 28:5-10). No words are eloquent enough, no mouth sufficient, no mind capable, no voice sweet enough, no body strong enough, no person dead or alive can possibly express but a faint shadow of the joy that is in store for us at the resurrection unto life eternal. On that blessed day, O Lord, I shall "depart quickly from the tomb with fear and joy!" Until then, Lord, I shall "run to tell" of your resurrection. Amen.

42. Easter Monday—First Commandment: *But I have trusted in your steadfast love; my heart shall rejoice in your salvation* (Psalm 13:5). O blessed Lord Jesus, who overcame death and the grave, grant that I may ever rejoice in your salvation, that I may have no other gods, and fear, love, and trust in you above all things; together

with the Father and the Holy Spirit. Amen.

43. Tuesday—Second Commandment: *Glory in his holy name; let the hearts of those who seek the Lord rejoice!* (Psalm 105:3). Gracious God, you have made known your holy and precious name in the sacred Scriptures. Grant that I may ever seek you, that I may forever rejoice in your name—Father, Son, and Holy Spirit! Amen.

44. Wednesday—Third Commandment: *And Hezekiah the king and the officials commanded the Levites to sing praises to the Lord with the words of David and of Asaph the seer. And they sang praises with gladness, and they bowed down and worshiped* (2 Chronicles 29:30). Almighty and everlasting God, Father, Son and Holy Spirit, grant that your Church may always rejoice in your Word, as did good king Hezekiah, that we may "regard it as sacred and gladly hear and learn it." Amen.

45. Thursday—Fourth Commandment: *Let your father and mother be glad; let her who bore you rejoice* (Proverbs 23:25). Father of all mercies, who sent your own dear Son to be my Savior, I thank you for my parents and the mercies which you have shown to me through them. Grant all parents increasing joy in their vocation, and cause children to "love and cherish" those through whom you blessed them with life; through Jesus Christ, our Lord. Amen.

46. Friday—Fifth Commandment: *You have loved righteousness and hated wickedness; therefore God, your God, has anointed you with the oil of gladness beyond your companions* (Hebrews 1:9). O Lord, you hate injustice and evil; you look upon the weak and hurting with compassion. Grant me a heart of gladness after your own, that I may speak for those who have no voice, champion the cause of the unborn, the disabled, and the aged, and demonstrate ready mercy and love in my daily life. Grant that injustice in our nation be corrected—that hearts may rejoice in you, your sacred gift of life, and in life eternal. In the name of the Father, the Son, and the Holy Spirit. Amen.

47. Saturday —Sixth Commandment: *Enjoy life with the wife*

whom you love, all the days of your vain life that he has given you under the sun, because that is your portion in life and in your toil at which you toil under the sun (Ecclesiastes 9:9). Grant, O Lord, joy and gladness to all Christian marriages, that husbands and wives may lead "sexually pure and decent lives in all they say and do." Grant all of us, married or not, joy in our vocation, that we may serve you with pure hearts; through Jesus Christ, our Lord. Amen.

Week of Easter 2 (Quasimodogeniti)

48. Sunday: *Like newborn infants, long for the pure spiritual milk, that by it you may grow up into salvation* (1 Peter 2:2). *For seven days you shall keep the feast to the Lord your God at the place that the Lord will choose, because the Lord your God will bless you in all your produce and in all the work of your hands, so that you will be altogether joyful* (Deuteronomy 16:15). O Lord, as we celebrate your blessed resurrection, cause us like newborn babes in the faith to take delight in our baptisms and your holy Word, that we may serve you in joy and gladness. Amen.

49. Monday—Seventh Commandment: *May he defend the cause of the poor of the people, give deliverance to the children of the needy, and crush the oppressor!* (Psalm 72:4). Gracious Lord, generous giver of all good things, preserve me from all greed, unkindness, and lack of charity, that I may find greater joy and gladness in a generous heart. Grant it, O Jesus! Amen.

50. Tuesday—Eighth Commandment: *I have no greater joy than to hear that my children are walking in the truth* (3 John 4). O God, giver of all good commands, cause me to repent where I fall short and to rejoice always in speaking the truth in love—defending, speaking well of, and putting the best meaning on everything. In Jesus, Amen.

51. Wednesday—Ninth Commandment: *God loves a cheerful giver. And God is able to make all grace abound to you, so that having all contentment in all things at all times, you may abound in every good*

work (2 Corinthians 9:7–8). Make me a happy, joyous, and cheerful giver, gracious God, by your blessed Gospel, so joyously delivered to me by your Son, my Savior, in whose name I pray. Amen.

52. Thursday—Tenth Commandment: *Everyone also to whom God has given wealth and possessions and power to enjoy them, and to accept his lot and rejoice in his toil—this is the gift of God* (Ecclesiastes 5:19). O Lord, fill my heart with joy in all your blessings to me, and drive far from me discontent, greed, and a joyless desire find true joy in anything other than you and your blessed Gospel, that I may rightly enjoy your other gifts; through Jesus Christ, our Lord. Amen.

53. Friday: *Let your mercy come to me, that I may live; for your law is my delight* (Psalm 119:77). Cause me, gracious Lord, to delight in your Law that I may depart from it neither to the left or right. Forgive my many failings, and establish me again on the narrow road by your mercy. Amen.

54. Saturday: *Just so, I tell you, there is joy before the angels of God over one sinner who repents* (Luke 15:10). Blessed Jesus, give me a repentant heart! May I always be a sinner! You dwell only in sinners! I cannot comprehend all of the angels rejoicing over me, but may they ever rejoice over me, and many, many others! Amen.

Week of Easter 3 (Misericordias Domini)

55. Sunday: *Shout for joy in the Lord, O you righteous! Praise befits the upright. Give thanks to the Lord with the lyre; make melody to him with the harp of ten strings! Sing to him a new song; play skillfully on the strings, with loud shouts. . . . The earth is full of the steadfast love of the Lord* (Psalm 33:1–3, 5). Eternal God, music is glorious enough in and of itself, but when it's set with joy to praise you in the resurrection of Christ, it reaches the goal of its creation. Bless the musicians this day as they increase our joy in you. Grant an increase of young, faithful, and joyous hearts who find joy in music sung and played—all to increase our joy in you; though Jesus Christ. Amen.

56. Monday—Creation: *Yet he did not leave himself without witness, for he did good by giving you rains from heaven and fruitful seasons, satisfying your hearts with food and gladness"* (Acts 14:17). O Lord, Creator of all things for my benefit, I praise you that the delights and delicacies of this earth are so wonderful to my eyes, so marvelous to taste, so heavenly to hear, giving me joy. Increase my joy sevenfold that I may receive my food and all delightful things, and know you, Father, Son, and Holy Spirit, as the giver of them all. Amen.

57. Tuesday—Redemption: *Go out from Babylon, flee from Chaldea, declare this with a shout of joy, proclaim it, send it out to the end of the earth; say, "The Lord has redeemed his servant Jacob!"* (Isaiah 48:20). Precious Savior of the Nations, you have redeemed the world "not with gold or silver" but with your "holy and precious blood." We are the redeemed among the nations. Now send us among the nations to all those for whom your blood was shed! And may we shout it with joy! Amen.

58. Wednesday—Conceived: *And Mary said, "My soul magnifies the Lord, and my spirit rejoices in God my Savior, for he has looked on the humble estate of his servant. For behold, from now on all generations will call me blessed; for he who is mighty has done great things for me, and holy is his name"* (Luke 1:46–49). Grant to me, dear Savior, the heart of Mary, who rejoiced in your humble conception, that I may find joy in your life as my very life's life. Amen.

59. Thursday—Born: *Fear not, for behold, I bring you good news of great joy that will be for all the people. For unto you is born this day in the city of David a Savior, who is Christ the Lord. And this will be a sign for you: you will find a baby wrapped in swaddling cloths and lying in a manger* (Luke 2:10–12). Gracious God, you caused the words "unto you" to be written for my comfort and consolation. Today I am a lowly shepherd, and I receive this Gospel with a glad heart; in the name of Jesus. Amen.

60. Friday—Suffered: *Therefore, since we are surrounded by so great*

a cloud of witnesses, let us also lay aside every weight, and sin which clings so closely, and let us run with endurance the race that is set before us, looking to Jesus, the founder and perfecter of our faith, who for the joy that was set before him endured the cross, despising the shame, and is seated at the right hand of the throne of God (Hebrews 12:1–2). Lord, grant that I may die to myself and the world that through every joy and sorrow, I may endure the cross, despise its shame, and look forward to eternal joys at your throne with Christ. Amen.

61. Saturday—Died and was buried: *Now may the God of peace who brought again from the dead our Lord Jesus, the great shepherd of the sheep, by the blood of the eternal covenant, equip you with everything good that you may do his will, working in us that which is pleasing in his sight, through Jesus Christ, to whom be glory forever and ever. Amen* (Hebrews 13:20–21). O Jesus, may we rejoice over nothing so much as knowing that you work in us that in which you delight—in death, through death, to life. Amen.

Week of Easter 4 (Jubilate)

62. Sunday: *Make a joyful noise to the Lord, all the earth; break forth into joyous song and sing praises!* (Psalm 98:4). *Your dead shall live; their bodies shall rise. You who dwell in the dust, awake and sing for joy! For your dew is a dew of light, and the earth will give birth to the dead* (Isaiah 26:19). Risen Christ, may every Easter hymn I sing, every absolution I hear, every account of the resurrection read, be for my soul a down payment of gladness unto joy everlasting. Amen.

63. Monday: *Go out from Babylon, flee from Chaldea, declare this with a shout of joy, proclaim it, send it out to the end of the earth; say, "The Lord has redeemed his servant Jacob!"* (Isaiah 48:20). I am redeemed by you, Gracious Lord. I am not my own; I have been bought with a price. I am precious in your sight, as precious as the very birth, life, death and resurrection of Jesus. O eternal joy! Amen and Amen!

64. Tuesday: *The God of hope fill you with all joy and peace in*

believing, so that by the power of the Holy Spirit you may abound in hope (Romans 15:13). Hope in you is the anchor of my joy, blessed Joy Eternal, Immanuel, Prince of Peace! By your Word, give me an extra measure of your Spirit that I may always hope and find joy in you! Amen.

65. Wednesday: Lord's Prayer—Introduction: Our Father who art in heaven—*May you be strengthened . . . with joy giving thanks to the Father, who has qualified you to share in the inheritance of the saints in light* (Colossians 1:11–12). A grateful heart is the reflection of joy. I thank you eternal Father, that you have granted your fatherhood to me in Christ. I am your beloved child and I rejoice! Amen.

66. Thursday: First Petition—Hallowed be thy name: *Glory in his holy name; let the hearts of those who seek the Lord rejoice!* (Psalm 105:3). In my baptism you placed your holy name upon me. You sought me in joy, that I might rejoice in seeking you. Grant, Lord, that I hallow your name in all that I believe and all that I do; in Jesus' name. Amen.

67. Friday: Second Petition—Thy kingdom come: *"The kingdom of heaven is like treasure hidden in a field, which a man found and covered up. Then in his joy he goes and sells all that he has and buys that field"* (Matthew 13:44). I sold myself as a slave to sin; now O Lord, I sell all to possess Christ, my precious treasure, my delight. Amen.

68. Saturday: Third Petition—Thy will be done: *And in every province and in every city, wherever the king's command and his edict reached, there was gladness and joy among the Jews, a feast and a holiday* (Esther 8:17). Give me a receptive and glad heart, O God, when I come into your presence. Through Jesus, make every Sunday an Easter, every Sunday a feast and holiday of gladness and joy. And cause my cold heart to burn with a passion for your every word. Amen.

Week of Easter 5 (Cantate)

69. Sunday: *Oh sing to the Lord a new song, for he has done marvelous things! His right hand and his holy arm have worked salvation for him. . . . Make a joyful noise to the Lord, all the earth; break forth into joyous song and sing praises! Sing praises to the Lord with the lyre, with the lyre and the sound of melody! With trumpets and the sound of the horn make a joyful noise before the King, the Lord!* (Psalm 98:1, 4–6). Such as I am, O God, I sing. I have but a weak voice, and so often find a sour note in my wretched life of self-chosen sin. But I sing in praise of your Gospel, nonetheless, for in Christ you hear only a "joyous song." Amen.

70. Monday: Fourth Petition—Give us this day our daily bread: *Go, eat your bread with joy, and drink your wine with a merry heart, for God has already approved what you do* (Ecclesiastes 9:7). *And day by day, attending the temple together and breaking bread in their homes, they received their food with glad and generous hearts* (Acts 2:46). God of all creation, you set before us daily a plenitude of flavors, textures, and colors. You supply foods from all nations, desserts that delight the tongue, wine (Psalm 104:15) that makes us smile and rejoice in our time with friends new and old. To be redeemed in Christ and also enjoy such gifts and goodness is supernal gladness. Amen.

71. Tuesday: Fifth Petition—Forgive us our trespasses as we forgive those who trespass against us: *"Blessed [happy!] are those whose lawless deeds are forgiven, and whose sins are covered* (Romans 4:7). It is extremely hard to forgive, O Lord, when I've been wronged or even slighted. Nothing so shows my self-centeredness as my unwillingness to forgive. Grant me mercy so that I may find greater joy in your forgiveness of my many sins, and cause that joy to spill out in love toward others who sin against me. Lord, I forgive _____ for the wrongs done and ask your forgiveness for my joyless, hardness of heart. Grant me a joyful, forgiving heart after your own. Amen.

72. Wednesday: Sixth Petition—Lead us not into temptation: *An evil man is ensnared in his transgression, but a righteous man sings*

and rejoices (Proverbs 29:6). Under the impartial glare of your Law, O God, I am unrighteous, sold as a slave to sin (Romans 6). The devil, the world, and my sinful flesh are heavy around my neck. Preserve me, Lord, from false belief, despair or other great shame and sins. And may every temptation drive me back to you for forgiveness, that I may sing and rejoice in Christ. Amen.

73. Thursday: Seventh Petition—But deliver us from evil: *When a woman is giving birth, she has sorrow because her hour has come, but when she has delivered the baby, she no longer remembers the anguish, for joy that a human being has been born into the world. So also you have sorrow now, but I will see you again, and your hearts will rejoice, and no one will take your joy from you* (John 16:21–22). You have promised, O Christ, that this valley of sorrows shall one day give way to an eternity of joy. Guard us from the devil and his tricks and from anything that would rob of us of true joy. Amen.

74. Friday: Conclusion—Amen: *Truly, truly [Amen, Amen], I say to you, you will weep and lament, but the world will rejoice. You will be sorrowful, but your sorrow will turn into joy* (John 16:20). Because you have anchored me in your future by not only a promise, but a double "Amen," dearest Jesus, I will rejoice right in the midst of my sorrow, knowing joy is assured. Amen.

75. Saturday—Baptism: *They were baptized by him in the river Jordan, confessing their sins* (Matthew 3:6). *For if while we were enemies we were reconciled to God by the death of his Son, much more, now that we are reconciled, shall we be saved by his life. More than that, we also rejoice in God through our Lord Jesus Christ, through whom we have now received reconciliation* (Romans 5:10–11). O God, you have combined your Word with water and made me your own. I confess my sin, and in Holy Absolution it is as though I've been baptized in the Jordan by John himself. Christ's death is mine, and so is his life. Grant me gladness for the day of my baptism! Amen.

Week of Easter 6 (Rogate)

76. Sunday: *Go out from Babylon, flee from Chaldea, declare this with a shout of joy, proclaim it, send it out to the end of the earth; say, "The Lord has redeemed his servant Jacob!"* (Isaiah 48:20). *Shout for joy to God, all the earth; sing the glory of his name; give to him glorious praise!* (Psalm 66:1–2). My shout is weak, my praise faint, my voice wavering, but I am redeemed! I shall shout it on my deathbed, though my voice be but a whisper of joy. Grant it, O Jesus! Amen.

77. Monday—Baptism: *Then I heard what seemed to be the voice of a great multitude, like the roar of many waters and like the sound of mighty peals of thunder, crying out, "Hallelujah! For the Lord our God the Almighty reigns"* (Revelation 19:6). *Repent and be baptized every one of you in the name of Jesus Christ for the forgiveness of your sins, and you will receive the gift of the Holy Spirit* (Acts 2:38). With the roar of baptismal waters, dousing "all nations" through all history, I rejoice to be one with you, O Christ, and with the whole Church. My sins are forgiven! The Holy Spirit is received! Hallelujah! Amen.

78. Tuesday—Baptism: *With joy you will draw water from the wells of salvation* (Isaiah 12:3). *And when Jesus was baptized, immediately he went up from the water, and behold, the heavens were opened to him, and he saw the Spirit of God descending like a dove and coming to rest on him; and behold, a voice from heaven said, "This is my beloved Son, with whom I am well pleased"* (Matthew 3:16–17). You placed yourself in the water, dearest Jesus, and I was placed in the water with you. I rejoice with you in the same Heavenly Father, who says to me, in you, "my beloved son!" Amen.

79. Wednesday—Baptism: *Christ loved the church and gave himself up for her, that he might sanctify her, having cleansed her by the washing of water with the word* (Ephesians 5:25–26). *I rejoice at your word* (Psalm 119:62). All the water on earth alone couldn't do such things, but the name "Father, Son, and Holy Spirit," together with the water makes it a water "life-giving, rich in grace, a washing

of new birth." With the water, "I rejoice at your word!" Amen.

80. Thursday—Ascension: *Then he led them out as far as Bethany, and lifting up his hands he blessed them. While he blessed them, he parted from them and was carried up into heaven. And they worshiped him and returned to Jerusalem with great joy, and were continually in the temple blessing God* (Luke 24:50–53). You departed from them, Jesus, and did they rejoice? Yet you ascended in order to "fill all things" (Ephesians 4:10). I rejoice on the road to Zion, though there be sorrow in the valley. In my baptism, you are always with me. Amen.

81. Friday—Baptism: *We were buried therefore with him by baptism into death, in order that, just as Christ was raised from the dead by the glory of the Father, we too might walk in newness of life* (Romans 6:4). *You have made known to me the paths of life; you will make me full of gladness with your presence* (Acts 2:20). How shall I live then, as baptized or not? So often I choose to live as though unwashed. Plunge me again into the waters of Confession and Absolution, and "make me full of gladness with your presence" through all the paths of my life, O Father, Son, and Holy Spirit, whose name I bear for eternity. Amen.

82. Saturday: *For you have died, and your life is hidden with Christ in God. . . . Christ is all, and in all . . . Put on then, as God's chosen ones, holy and beloved, compassionate hearts, kindness, humility, meekness, and patience . . . And let the peace of Christ rule in your hearts, to which indeed you were called in one body. And be thankful . . . And whatever you do, in word or deed, do everything in the name of the Lord Jesus, giving thanks to God the Father through him* (Colossians 3:3, 11–17). O Jesus, I have died with you. Be my all in all, and give me a joyous and thankful heart, gracious to all. Amen.

Week of Easter 7 (Exaudi)

83. Sunday: *Hear, O Lord, when I cry aloud; be gracious to me and answer me! . . . The Lord is my light and my salvation; whom shall I fear? The Lord is the stronghold of my life; of whom shall I be afraid? . . . And now my head shall be lifted up above my enemies all around me, and I will offer in his tent sacrifices with shouts of joy; I will sing and make melody to the Lord* (Psalm 27:7, 1, 6). The sacrifice of joy shall mark my life, O Lord! Joy in you! Joy in suffering, joy in plenty, joy in the midst of sorrow, joy in your forgiveness, joy in my life with others, joy at my last hour, joy forever and ever. God grant it for Jesus' sake! Amen.

84. Monday: *"This is my body, which is given for you. Do this in remembrance of me." . . . "This cup that is poured out for you is the new covenant in my blood"* (Luke 22:19–20). *They feast on the abundance of your house, and you give them drink from the river of your delights* (Psalm 36:8). Precious Lamb of God, who takes away the sin of the world, I do not understand it. I cannot comprehend it. I cannot explain it. I cannot fathom it. Yet, by your grace I believe it. You give me your very body and blood to eat and to drink. I delight to come to your table. Amen.

85. Tuesday: *Peter said to them, "Repent and be baptized every one of you in the name of Jesus Christ for the forgiveness of your sins, and you will receive the gift of the Holy Spirit* (Acts 2:38). *But the fruit of the Spirit is love, joy, peace, patience, kindness, goodness, faithfulness, gentleness, self-control; against such things there is no law.* (Galatians 5:22–23). O Holy Spirit, Eternal Fire, kindle your flame in my cold, hard, sad heart, and grant your precious gifts—above all, joy. You live and reign with the Father and the Son, one God, evermore. Amen.

86. Wednesday: *Whatever prayer, whatever plea is made by any man or by all your people Israel, each knowing the affliction of his own heart and stretching out his hands toward this house, then hear . . . and forgive . . . On the eighth day [Solomon] sent the people away, and they*

blessed the king and went to their homes joyful and glad of heart for all the goodness that the Lord had shown to David his servant and to Israel his people (1 Kings 8:38, 39, 66). O Jesus, just as Solomon once pointed his people to the altar of the great Temple and its sacrifices for forgiveness, may we with joyful and glad hearts receive your body and blood, bless the king, and go home happily. For you have told us directly that the "benefit of such eating and drinking" is receiving the sacrifice "given and shed for you." Amen.

87. Thursday: *Therefore, brothers, since we have confidence to enter the holy place by the blood of Jesus . . . let us draw near with a true heart in full assurance of faith, with our hearts sprinkled clean from an evil conscience. . . . Let us hold fast the confession of our hope. . . . And let us consider how to stir up one another to love and good works, not neglecting to meet together. . . . But recall the former days when . . . you endured a hard struggle with sufferings. . . . For you had compassion on those in prison, and you joyfully accepted the plundering of your property, since you knew that you yourselves had a better possession and an abiding one* (Hebrews 10:19ff.). O Lord, we have no idea how bodily eating and drinking can "do such great things." But in your blessed Sacrament, sprinkle our hearts clean from all sin and troubles of conscience. Stir us to love one another and to find joy in gathering to receive your gifts. May we joyfully sacrifice all to be found in you, with the Father and the Holy Spirit, one God. Amen.

88. Friday: *And they devoted themselves to the apostles' teaching and the fellowship, to the breaking of bread and the prayers. . . . And they were selling their possessions and belongings and distributing the proceeds to all, as any had need. And day by day, attending the temple together and breaking bread in their homes, they received their food with glad and generous hearts, praising God and having favor with all the people. And the Lord added to their number day by day those who were being saved* (Acts 2:42ff.). The Church of the apostles rejoiced in fellowship with the Father through You, O Christ, and in fellowship with one another in faith, prayer, the Sacraments, and works

of love (Smalcald Articles II IV 9). Grant that your body and blood may make us ever more your mystical Body, the Church, and that we love one another with tireless joy and gladness, and that through us also, you may add many to the number of the saved. Amen.

89. Saturday: *So also you have sorrow now, but I will see you again, and your hearts will rejoice, and no one will take your joy from you. In that day you will ask nothing of me. Truly, truly, I say to you, whatever you ask of the Father in my name, he will give it to you. Until now you have asked nothing in my name. Ask, and you will receive, that your joy may be full* (John 16:22–24). Lord of all joy, gracious source of all eternal pleasure and happiness, you are pleased when I am joyous in you. You promise to hear and grant my prayer. I ask one thing, and one thing only. Grant me joy in you and in you to the full; you who live and reign with the Father and the Spirit, one God, now and forever. Amen.

Pentecost

90. Sunday—Pentecost: *And there you shall eat before the Lord your God, and you shall rejoice, you and your households, in all that you undertake, in which the Lord your God has blessed you* (Deuteronomy 12:7). Grant me joy this day in your house, and cause that joy to abound in my home, until I shall rest in your eternal home. Amen! Amen! Amen!

> "*Therefore we are comforted. And besides our own comfort, we rejoiced still more . . .*" 2 CORINTHIANS 7:13